# Collecting now
*Care and repair of your antiques*

# Collecting Now

*Care and repair of your antiques*

John FitzMaurice Mills

ARIEL BOOKS

BRITISH BROADCASTING CORPORATION

Drawings by Chris Evans

Acknowledgement is due to the following for permission to reproduce certain photographs in this book:

British Museum, page viii

Ciba-Geigy Ltd, pages iii, iv, v, vi, vii, ix (*bottom*), xi (*top*), xiii

The remaining photographs are the author's copyright

Published by the
British Broadcasting Corporation
35 Marylebone High Street
London W1M 4AA

ISBN 0 563 20126 6

Originally published in hardback as *Look After your Antiques* by Ebury Press
© John FitzMaurice Mills and The National Magazine Company Ltd. 1980
Revised and enlarged edition first published 1982
Reprinted 1983
© John FitzMaurice Mills 1982

Printed in England by Mackays of Chatham
This book is set in 10 on 11 point Ehrhardt Linotron

# Contents

# Warning Note
## Dealing with Chemicals

A number of chemicals and mixtures are virtually indispensable to the restorer of antiques. Many of them have been in household use in former years, and provided you handle them sensibly there is no need to fight shy of them. The main points to remember are: *keep all chemicals out of the eyes and mouth and off the skin*; don't spread chemicals around the house; be on your guard against setting chemicals on fire. The general safety rules given below should be followed whenever such substances are used or stored in the home.

### Poisonous and corrosive substances
The most poisonous chemical mentioned is oxalic acid; the most corrosive are 5% nitric or sulphuric acids and sodium hydroxide (caustic soda). All these should be handled with care, as indicated. However, *all are easily washed off with water*. If an accident should happen, despite all precautions, run to the tap before deciding if any further treatment is needed. Keep these substances, and any mixture containing them, away from the very young, the old, whose sight may be failing, and household pets.

### Inflammables
Several of the mixtures mentioned and many proprietary products contain inflammable liquids.

| Substance | Risk factor |
| --- | --- |
| Benzine, hexane and petroleum ether | Related to petrol and just as dangerous |
| Alcohol, methylated spirits and acetone | Equally inflammable |
| White spirit, paraffin, turpentine and linseed oil | Slightly less inflammable – except when they are heated |

The precautions are obvious: *don't smoke or work near a naked flame*; if you must use large quantities, *work outside*.

## Handling liquids

Splashing or spillage are the hazards. Get into the habit of keeping your face away from liquids. Protect your eyes with glasses, sunglasses or goggles.

Remove the cork or cap at arm's length; any internal pressure may spray a little liquid out when you open the bottle.

Pour liquids carefully, again at arm's length, away from your eyes. Don't slop them about. Replace the cork or cap securely and wipe off any drips with a rag or tissue. *Never lift bottles by the cap.*

Plan beforehand how to cope with any spillage. Rags or old newspapers are ideal for mopping up and can go straight into the dustbin.

## Mixing

In most cases where solutions or mixtures are needed, we have advised readers to ask their local chemist to make them up. However you may need to do it yourself. None of the 'recipes' need to be followed with scientific precision – cookery standards will suffice.

Many solids take some time and stirring to get them to dissolve. Others require the liquid to be warmed. The only safe way to heat inflammable liquids is to *put the loosely closed container in a bowl of hot water, away from naked flames and preferably out of doors.*

Some recipes specify a 'saturated solution'; this simply means one that contains as much solid as will dissolve, given time and stirring.

## Check-list for using chemicals

1 Choose a suitable workplace, with enough room and good ventilation; take precautions against possible spillage.

2 Read the instructions for proprietary products. Spray liquids with care, and note that scrubbing with a liquid will itself produce a spray. Protect your eyes in both cases.

3 When possible, work on a small scale, so that you risk only small accidents. When you must work on a larger scale, for example, white spirit by the trayful for cleaning textiles, or buckets of ammonia or caustic soda solution, take special care and move outdoors.

4 Avoid splashing caused by accidentally dropping something such as a brush into a bucket of chemicals. *Be particularly careful when totally immersing an object in a dangerous liquid.* Devise and test a method of lifting and lowering the article safely: perhaps

with wooden laundry tongs or in a string bag, or simply with string through the handle, if there is a strong one. Again, *protect the eyes from splashes.*

## Storing chemicals
Label all ingredients and mixtures clearly.

Keep chemicals in securely closed special containers, not in household bottles or tins where they could be mistaken for groceries, in a place inaccessible to the very young or the old.

# Introduction

Antiques can be made from an unsuspected variety of materials: metals of almost every kind, countless different woods, animal and plant fibres, clay, stone, painted and enamelled surfaces, glass, papier mâché, horn, precious and semi-precious gems, amber, tortoiseshell and other exotic and strange materials which the craftsman has at some time used. The objects may be carefully jointed, stuck together with animal and fish glues, riveted with iron or copper, glazed, varnished, polished and burnished. Most of which makes them liable to attack from several directions.

In the past, antiques will have had to contend with damp, devouring insects, sun streaming in through windows, careless handling, the odd fire and flood. Most of these hazards they seem to have withstood quite well, even surviving the attentions of over-keen or ignorant restorers. But today's way of life has brought further reinforcements for the destructors.

**Over-dry atmosphere**
Probably the single greatest danger comes from our love of comfort, of having the home at times turned almost into a hothouse. Warmth if introduced gradually can be all right, but if, come the first parky draughts of late autumn, the central heating is brought in with a rush and overnight the temperature of the house is given a twenty or thirty degree boost, and to this are added the effects of an over-enthusiastic air-conditioning plant, which really puts the boot in by lowering the relative humidity (the moisture content of the air) by thirty or more per cent, then trouble can be on the way. Solid oak Tudor furniture that has resisted the rough and tumble of hundreds of years of family life can split, leather upholstery will lose its substance and strength, glues can desiccate and a whole range of our precious and rare possessions can be put in jeopardy.

The first step to solving the problem is quite simple: have a little patience. When the heating is switched on, bring up the temperature gradually over a week or ten days; this will allow all the different substances to adjust. Air-conditioning needs watching, for it will not only affect your possessions but also you. It is worth spending a few pounds to buy a hygrometer, a gadget that will measure the relative humidity. The most beneficial figure to aim for, not only for antiques but also for yourselves, is around 60–65%.

If the atmosphere is over-dry invest in a humidifier. The simplest and cheapest of these is a water-containing affair that can be hung on a radiator or placed near a source of heat. These may be earthenware, metal or plastic, it does not matter which, and all they need is a regular topping up with water. More efficient types will be operated electrically with a reservoir of water and be controlled by their own hygrometer. This can be set to give the desired humidity which will be adhered to by the appliance emitting atomised water into the atmosphere.

### Insect pests

Next on the list of would-be destroyers come the insects, which vary in destructive power according to district, country and type. Some people unfortunately imagine that these nasties only attack wood. Regrettably, not so. On their menu are also the following: textiles, leather, paper, cardboard, glues and sometimes other animal substances. The first line of defence here is regular inspection. Spring is a time in particular to watch, as this is when the pests will be on the move. It may sound a bore, but be thorough. A little time spent routing around in corners and cracks can often stop an incipient attack before too much damage has been done. It may then be possible to deal with by a simple home-applied treatment rather than having to bring in the professionals. If you do need an all-out fumigation and impregnation this should include a lengthy guarantee period.

### Dry rot

When on the hunt for insect pests, watch out for any signs of that sly destroyer, dry rot. Often its presence can be detected by picking up a slightly sour, stale smell. The trouble is that, especially in older properties, it tends to start its depredations in the most awkward places; under floorboards, under stairs, the undersides of shelves in cupboards set into stone walls and the like. Dry rot can be recognised in the earlier stages as a white, fluffy, cotton wool-like mass that spreads out over the wood like a silky white sheet. It may also appear with a pearly-grey colour and splodges of pale mauve and lemon yellow.

What dry rot does not like is ventilation; it will tend to establish itself and flourish where there are pockets of stagnant air and an over-humid atmosphere. Inspect ventilation bricks outside the building to see that they have not become blocked with debris from flower beds. If the house that you are moving into has that muggy, stale feel about it get a builder to go round with you and if any dank corners are found, take some remedial measures to ensure some ventilation can reach them. Dry rot unfortunately will not confine itself just to the fabric of a building. Even small draughts can spread the spore dust which is very light and of a reddish-brown colour. Thus furniture such as wardrobes, bulky desks and dressers can become victims if they are in positions which have stagnant and damp atmospheres. If this unpleasant thing is discovered, it should be treated by a professional, and most firms offering this service will give a guaranteed period of immunity after the treatment.

## Wet rot

With older property, wet rot may also be encountered, although the causative degree of dampness is not very often found. Here the early signals can be a darkening of the wood surface; then, as the attack develops, the wood tends to break into cubical pieces. It is important to trace the source of the moisture that is encouraging the outbreak. This may be a faulty damp-proof course, a leaking pipe joint or perished flashing. If the source is found and stopped and the wet rot has got no further than the darkening stage, it may be quite simply treated by one of the proprietary preparations that can be bought from the ironmonger or builders' merchant.

This fighting of damp in your house is vital for the long life of many of the pieces you may have. It is not only wood that can suffer but also objects with cane, rushes, papier mâché, cardboards, leather, textiles and metals in their construction. Rots and rust, once they take a hold, are mighty persistent and often, even when eradicated, can leave behind stained, cracked and pitted surfaces.

## Condensation

In this foray against moisture there is one other source that can be overlooked, which can produce quite astonishing amounts of dampness, that is condensation. The cause is nearly always poor ventilation and large cold surfaces, such as stone, metal, ceramic tiles and the like. In old houses with chimneys and fireplaces in nearly every room there is not much likelihood of the condition but with today's chimneyless houses it is important to see that some ventilation is being provided, either by a window or perforated brick or block. Watch out too for steam from cooking or clothes drying, which has no means of escape. Houses shut up for a period, however limited, can develop condensation to a degree that will affect polished wood surfaces and cause mould growths on textiles, leather and other susceptible substances.

### Over-exposure to light

Sunlight contains ultra-violet rays which can be harmful and with fragile objects quite disastrous if they are over-exposed. With paintings, certain pigments can fade and change and varnish films may crack. Wood in fine furniture can be bleached and have the patina of the years ruined. Many textiles will fade almost out of recognition and if the relative humidity is over-high, even seemingly strong fibres will perish and rot.

Whenever possible the play of direct sunlight on to furniture, paintings – particularly water-colours – fabrics, leathers, woods – especially veneers – and other delicate works of art, should be avoided. For a very precious piece of embroidery or lace there is a special glass that has been treated to exclude a high percentage of the harmful rays. There is a clear varnish containing an ingredient that inhibits ultra-violet rays that can be brushed over the inside surfaces of skylights or windows; it may also be applied to the glazing in frames.

Artificial light, too, may emit ultra-violet rays, particularly fluorescent tubes and, to a much lesser degree, tungsten lamps. Adequate illumination is a must but don't over-illuminate. Some high power tungsten bulbs can generate considerable heat that will cause damage by desiccation and scorching. Bouncing light from the ceiling is worth experimenting with and often surprisingly successful results can be had that are not only safe for antiques but are also very pleasant to live with.

### Travelling hazards

Daylight, relative humidity and temperature change can have much more effect on antiques than might be imagined. Everywhere now it seems things are being collected and thus those prize pieces of craftsmanship, and even quite humble objects, are joining the 'jet set' and spending more and more of their time crossing atmosphere lines. Maybe from such as the steamy air of parts of India to the dry-as-a-bone atmosphere of North Africa. In places like Australia the difference in humidity between various areas may be 30 or 40%. A good little oak joint-stool may have lived happily in a Cornish home for 300 years, changed hands through a dealer and found itself a few weeks later in Chicago in the late fall. Suddenly it may be subjected to 95% humidity and then as the windows are shut and the air-conditioning switched on, there is a drop in a matter of an hour or two to around 35%. Result, horrible internal reactions and something is probably going to have to give.

If you have anything of worth or that is at all fragile, please give it a thought before moving. Experienced removal men should be competent, and, insurance covered or not, keep an eye on matters. If doing the job oneself, the main points to watch for are to provide a cushion against movement, the concussion of a hard knock or possible drop; rigidity where called for, and protection as far as possible from sudden heat change; also have a weatherproof covering.

## Polluted air

Our progressive 20th century has stacked up another category of risk for our beloved antiques, and, sadly, apart from a few surface protective measures, it is one that little can be done about. Air pollution is something that started with coal fires and then burgeoned with the massive increase of chemical manufacturing processes, the four-wheeled steeds and other little conveniences of life. Steps are being taken, laws passed and certainly in some areas progress has been made.

The incomplete combustion of fuels, the burning of wastes, and vast industrial activities spread millions of tons of pollutants into the air and thus down on to us and ours. We get gritty throats and uncomfortable eyes. The antiques? Their ailments may take longer to show up. Delicate patinas, paint films, fine wood surfaces, polished metals and fragile fabrics can become layered with microscopic droplets of some obnoxious chemical or covered with abrasive dusts from a cement factory or similar industrial concern.

The worst of these villains is sulphur dioxide, which belts out from many different sources; it meets moisture and becomes acid. It will attack most things. Marble statuary will stain and the surface be eaten into, leather weakens, papers become brittle, metals tarnish and pit. All one can do as a first line of defence is to practise good husbandry. Dust off abrasive mess and apply polishes or lacquers to give some protective coating.

## Vibration

One last cause of damage to our precious and rare, and that is vibration. Heavy traffic, particularly in towns where there is much starting and stopping, can kick up movement in buildings which can quite easily be felt. The older establishments by their massive solidity seem to withstand this the best. But even they will transmit vibration waves.

Under this heading comes the sonic boom of those faster-than-fast machines. Only those who live down the flight paths are at risk. It can be powerful in effect, for there is at least one little baroque church in Bavaria which can show a seriously cracked dome, and not very long ago I was working on a large Niccolò dell' Abbate in a château just to the south of the Loire near Blois, when a flight of very hurried French airforce went over. Booming away they cracked the ceiling and showered me and the Abbate with a liberal quantity of debris.

# Furniture

The patina of fine polished woods has an appeal all of its own. A good stout oak table from the 17th century must have had hundreds of polishes to build up that mellow tone. The colours have a semi-translucence under the shielding coats of wax. For many it is this finish brought up by countless hands over the years which is so attractive and should wherever possible be preserved. Each kind of tree lends itself to the skill of the craftsman and there are many that have been used, all of them having certain individual characteristics. Below is a list of some of the woods that have been used either as solid wood or veneer.

## An ABC of cabinetmakers' woods

*Abricotier*
The wood of the apricot tree, hard with a yellowish tint, a favourite with the French *ébénistes* (cabinet-makers who specialised in making veneered furniture, so called because ebony was used in the earliest veneered furniture in France).

*Acacia faux*
From the common locust tree, hard with a clear yellow and green stripe.

*Agalloch*
East Indian tree. It is the aloes of the Bible and in the Far East is burnt to produce a perfume. Also known as agila-wood and eagle-wood.

*Ailanthus*
In the Moluccas known as the 'tree of Heaven', because of the

great height to which it grows, it is hard with a reddish veined appearance.

*Amaranth*
From Guyana, it has a rich purple-red colour and is used widely in cabinetwork.

*Amboyna*
Native of the Moluccas (the Spice Islands), hard with a distinctive rose-yellow-brown tint, mottled with curling. Popular for veneers.

*Apple*
Cultivated or wild, pink-brown shades, equally good for veneer, carving or turning, popular with British and American cabinetmakers.

*Beech*
Hard, with at times very pale tones.

*Birch*
Hard, close-grained, pale in colour and sometimes stained to imitate mahogany. A North American variety was imported into England during the late 18th century. Used for spindles, legs and whole framework of chairs, as well as veneers.

*Bog*
Wood of trees preserved in peat bogs, having a shiny black look resembling ebony. Bog oak is the most common; pine and fir (deal) have also been found. In Elizabeth I's time used for inlay.

*Box*
Very hard and close-grained, pale ochre in colour, used for inlays, particularly long thin strips to protect edges of veneering.

*Caliatour*
An East Indian hard red dye-wood very popular with cabinet-makers.

*Campêche*
A kind of mahogany, a hard and reddish brown dye-wood. It is also called logwood.

*Cannelle*
From the West Indies and Ceylon, hard and nearly white; the wild cinnamon.

*Cedar*
There are several trees that come under this name: Cedar of Lebanon, North American red cedar, a West Indian species, and other varieties from Australia, Japan, Mexico and New Zealand. Durable with a soothing fragrance, often used for making chests.

*Châtaignier*
Wood from the chestnut, hard and pale yellow.

*Cherry*
Quite hard with a warm reddish colour and used for inlay and small items.

*China tree*
The azedarac, also known as chinaberry, bead tree, holy tree, pride of India and Indian lilac. From China and Guyana, hard and black speckled, red-brown colour.

*Citron*
Wood of the sandarac, hard and pale with veining and a lingering fragrance; from Morocco.

*Courbaril*
West Indian locust tree, hard and pale red, with veining.

*Cypress*
A number of varieties, they are mostly hard and pale red with a warm brown veining. Much used for statuary by the Ancients.

*Deal*
Not a type on its own. Wood cut from fir or pine trees.

*Ebony*
From tropical Africa and Asia, extremely hard and durable, of an intense black, it will take a very high polish. Some of the best came from Madagascar.

*Elm*
Hard and strong, used for some furniture and domestic implements.

*Fusain*
Hard and pale yellow, this was popular with the French *ébénistes*; the tree is also known as the Spindle tree.

*Hickory*
An American hardwood similar to Australian featherwood.

*Holly*
Fine-grained, hard pale wood. Used with marquetry and inlay.

*Jacaranda*
South American tree, very hard with an unusual black and near-white blotchy look.

*King-wood*
A Brazilian wood, also termed violet wood after the colour of the markings.

*Laburnum*
Sought after for veneer work, especially the slicer cuts across a branch to produce an 'oyster shell' pattern.

*Lignum vitae*
One of the hardest of all woods, from the Guaiacum family of trees found in the West Indies and tropical South America. Dark coloured, it has been used for veneers but is more often found turned into bowls and some drinking vessels.

*Mahogany*
The most popular wood for fine furniture, from Dominican, Cuban and Jamaican forests. Its use on a large scale dates from about 1720. Very compact, it will rarely shrink or warp and is not greatly affected by changes in temperature and humidity.

*Maple*
Hard, light coloured, close grained often with curly and 'bird's eye' veining.

*Oak*
Hard and compact with pleasant light colour in the raw state, the most important wood for Medieval, Renaissance, Tudor and Jacobean furniture in those periods in England, Flanders and Germany.

*Olive*
A hard, close-grained wood with exciting veining, popular from the time of the early Egyptians.

*Pine*
Any tree of the genus *Pinus,* pale yellow, mostly used for the carcass for veneers, also to carry gesso and gilding, often left plain and waxed or varnished.

*Rosewood*
The wood from several trees from Brazil, Honduras and India. Hard with rich colours and streaking.

*Sandalwood*
From the East Indies, warm yellow ochre colour with pleasant fragrance, often used for chests and drawers.

*Teak*
An East Indian tree, hard and notably resistant to damp and decay, yellow-brown.

*Tulip-wood*
The wood of the tulip tree; from Brazil, it ages to a warm, pleasant yellow.

*Walnut*
One of the favourites with the craftsmen of the Restoration. It has interesting veining and also yields 'oyster shells' from branch slices.

*Zebra-wood*
From Guyana, French Guiana and Surinam; hard with a strong striping.

This list of woods could probably be trebled or more if all the timbers the cabinetmakers had experimented with were included. To those must be added a strange motley of materials that were used as inlays, marquetry and applied decoration. These include bone, ivory, horn, tortoiseshell, mother-of-pearl, ceramic plaques, bronze, copper, steel, silver and brass. The cabinetmakers had great skill with joints using dowel pins and, later, screws and sometimes handmade nails. They made up their glues from hooves, horns, fish gelatine, rabbit skins and other similar materials. All of which in their day led up to a fairly high degree of permanence, whether working with solid wood or carcass and veneers. Bearing all this in mind, when something starts to go wrong, with today's conditions it can present a fairly complex problem. The arm of a Jacobean chair splits. What do you do? Please, not what often is done. This is to screw a chunk of metal plate on the underside with oversize screws, just making more trouble for the future. If the chair is of value, take it to a trained man. The joints of a Charles II wingback chair start to loosen. Don't try forcing in wedges in incorrect places. Give it to a professional. If veneers seriously lift in large areas, leave this also to a skilled man.

These antiques are precious whether they are in the top rank or a truthful stripped pine from the old sheep farmer's kitchen. But there is much that you, as the trustee for this period, can do and suggested below are some of the materials that can be used and some processes that if used carefully should bring no harm; in fact, they can do much good for the life of these things we live with. But do watch as whatever you are doing proceeds, and if anything untoward starts to happen, stop, and bring in the professional.

## Materials, problems and processes

### Adhesives

The choice here can be confusing as the facts about each type tend to become a bit muddled with all the advertising jargon. Where possible it is really the best practice to use a glue that can, if something goes wrong, or if someone at a later date wishes to re-do the restoration, be reversed. Animal and fish glues are fairly simple to detach. Many of the synthetic adhesives will require solvents such as acetone to make them loosen their grip; this may be all right, but there could be some sensitive materials close by that could be attacked by this liquid. Really each problem needs individual consideration at the time it is tackled. If using synthetics, take care to avoid dropping them on to any surfaces not being treated, as some dry very quickly and can be difficult to remove. (See PRODUCTS.)

### Basketwork

Whether made into a complete piece of furniture or incorporated as a part, it needs a watchful eye. The woodworm can be partial to it as an appetizer, both with the weave and the strengthening members. If an attack is noticed, take the object outside and give it a liberal soaking with one of the proprietary woodworm killing liquids (see PRODUCTS), being sure that all areas are reached; then leave under cover, but not in the house, for several days to allow the liquid to evaporate completely.

Weaknesses are quite common where the members of the weave bend back on themselves and also, of course, where the worm has had a go. To put some strength back into the piece, prepare a mixture of one part acrylic matt medium, obtainable from an art shop, with one part water and with this again liberally soak the areas to be treated. A second and third application may be made to be sure of the job. When this has dried off, give the whole object a coat of high quality white polish (again, see PRODUCTS); leave for about two hours and then buff up.

## Beeswax polish

If you have the time and a suitable place to work, you can make up your own traditional polish like that which must have been used for centuries and that somehow seems in sympathy with fine woods. *Warning*: There is a fire hazard as turpentine and white spirit are inflammable. Melt 25 g (1 oz) beeswax over a low flame, and when it is completely liquid, turn out all flames and stir in 75 ml (3 fl oz) turpentine or white spirit.

The nice thing about doing this is that you can produce your own excellent polishes ranging from a really stiff consistency, by using less turpentine, to a light cream, by adding more turpentine. Broadly speaking, a stiff polish is best suited to a solid wood, such as oak or elm, and a light cream to veneers, where the extra punch with the polishing of a stiff paste could cause a bit of lifting if any areas were at all loose.

Beeswax polish has with it some of the magic of the bees, as it is highly resistant to mould growths and also it is unlikely to bloom or be greatly affected by damp. Further, unlike some of the modern aerosol polishes that shall be nameless, it is quite harmless if the cat wants to lick it or walks on it and licks his paws afterwards.

## Bleaching, to remedy

This is generally brought on by prolonged exposure to sunlight; it may take some years before it shows up. The wood will need feeding to bring back the substance to the top layers and surface. Teak oil (see PRODUCTS) can be a helpful revivifier. This can be applied in the form of a liquid or a foam with a piece of cotton wool and rubbed well into the grain; then leave for two days, examine and if necessary repeat the dose. As the colour and correct tone starts to come back, a good wax polish will foster the recovery. If possible it is better to resist the temptation of putting on water-soluble or other wood dyes as it is very easy to end up with an artificial look that will be very difficult if not impossible to remove.

## Bloom, to remove

An unsightly condition that can come up on some wax polished wood surfaces, and also with lacquered and varnished finishes. What the exact cause of it is, is arguable. It has the appearance of a soft grey blush rather like the bloom on a grape. Some say that it is brought on by a polishing done on a cold, damp day; others that the surface may have been slightly damp when the polish, lacquer or varnish was applied. It is unsightly but can generally be easily removed by a light application of a good white wax polish (see PRODUCTS). Other remedies include rubbing over with slightly warmed turpentine (see WARNING NOTE) or a small amount of oil of spike, obtainable from a chemist or herbalist, the lavender scent of which is pleasant.

## Bone

This may be found in inlays and quite often forming the escutcheon plates round the keyholes on chests of drawers and desks. If they become loose, it is best to stick them down again with an animal or fish glue (see PRODUCTS). Synthetic adhesives can sometimes be highly penetrating and could pass through to the external surface. With a scalpel or small knife blade, scrape off all traces of the earlier glue from the bone, and also from the depression in which it had rested. With a cotton bud dipped in methylated spirits, give the back of the bone a wipe and likewise the depression; this is to be sure that there is no grease present. Place the drawer so that the front is uppermost and apply the heated animal or fish glue to the depression, press in the bone escutcheon, wipe off any excess glue that is extruded, place a small piece of clean cloth over the bone and leave it to set with a flat-iron to keep it down.

## Boulle

That attractive type of marquetry which was developed by André Charles Boulle with other members of his family. No one quite equalled him with his handling of metals and tortoiseshell. He left one tricky point for the collector as he never signed his work and actual pieces of Boulle that can be certified as his work are rare. Under normal conditions of use and environment these acts of genius seem to have survived quite well. But the bringing of them into atmospheres controlled by central heating and air-conditioning is wreaking havoc in all too many cases. The thin slivers of metal become loose and are then caught by a carelessly applied polishing cloth and there is trouble. To a lesser degree the tortoiseshell will also come up and get pulled off. If the piece is a genuine or 'near miss' Boulle, unquestionably reach for the phone and call your expert. For here is a task that can take a long time; it may need impregnation, and it is more than likely that the whole surface will have to be gone over if the areas of disintegration are widespread.

But if there are only some very small fragments coming away and the commode is a splendid reproduction from the craftshops of the late 19th century, have a try with care. The tortoiseshell will be best reseated with an animal glue (see PRODUCTS), possibly rabbit-skin is best, as it is almost colourless. As with the bone escutcheons, make sure all the old adhesive is removed and all surfaces to be stuck together are degreased. Try to arrange that some firm pressure can be applied whilst the tortoiseshell is setting.

The metal strips are not quite so simple. It is likely that when the maker put them in place he used some secret recipe with shellac, fish glue and varnish. This will not be easy to concoct. So use a synthetic adhesive sparingly, and select one that will take to both wooden and metal surfaces, again taking care that no excess spreads across the outside surface.

## Bruises and abrasions, to reduce

If these are severe and there is any really noticeable denting there is not really much that you can do. But if the damage is slight or it is in the nature of scratching it should be possible to lessen the defect. Proprietary scratch removers (see PRODUCTS) will suffice for light abrasions; all that most of these do is to slightly dissolve the layers of wax polish and thus produce what appears to be a smooth surface. Depending on the value of the piece, you can try a little heat and moisture. This should be done with care. First, with some turpentine or white spirit, wipe off excess polish from the area to be treated for bruising. Now lay a couple of thicknesses of damp cloth over the damage and apply an iron set at the lowest setting; hold it in place for about 30 seconds, lift off and examine progress. Repeat several times, with pauses in between so that the wood does not get too hot.

If you have such a thing, an electric spatula will do the job best as by its small size the heated area will be minimised. After treatment, let the piece dry right off and then repolish.

## Burns and scorches, to disguise

Here again, if the object has value, turn the matter over to the pro. But if of a lesser nature you can try. Burns and scorches where there is blackening of the area are one of the trickiest problems to restore with antiques of any type. This is mainly because the substance of the material attacked will have changed. If the burn is not too deep, a gentle rubbing of the affected part with an abrasive such as crocus powder (see GLOSSARY), powdered cuttle fish or a fine emery powder, using a finger, may do the trick. Stop every so often and watch progress. Afterwards feed the wood with teak oil (see PRODUCTS) and then repolish. Try not to be tempted to use anything so drastic as coarse sandpaper, a file or metal scraper. The result can look far worse than scorches left showing.

## Canework

Normally found on the seats and backs of chairs it is a resilient and long lasting material. If it does begin to look a little shabby it may be washed with a weak solution of soap and water; rinse this well away afterwards and allow to dry. Weak areas can be given a consolidation with the acrylic medium and water mixture suggested for basketwork. To bring back the lustre of the cane, never use varnish, as the conjunction of this with a warm posterior, even after the varnish has seemingly dried right out, can be embarrassing for a shy guest. The better course is to dissolve a little purified bleached beeswax in benzine and rub this into the cane, leave for about an hour and then buff up with a soft cloth or woolpad. *Warning*: benzine, a form of petrol, is highly inflammable.

## Cracks, to fill

These may occur in solid wood or with veneered furniture where the carcass has moved and torn the veneer (see photograph). They need treating as they will soon fill with grime which not only looks unpleasant but can also give the 'come-on' to a Mrs Woodworm who is looking for somewhere to lay her eggs. As far as possible clean out the small crevices. If they are quite small they can be filled with beeswax. This can be gently warmed until plastic and then various dry powder colours, obtainable from an art shop, can be kneaded into it to match the wood. If the cracks are a bit on the large side it may be better to use one of the commercial 'fillers'. If this is done, fill so that it lies a little bit below the surface, and when it is hard, finish off with some of the tinted wax, as this will help to give a more natural look when the area is repolished.

## Dyes
A wide selection of water and spirit dyes is available to match most of the woods commonly used. A word of warning though. They can be excellent if used with some skill and experience, but once on, they are there, so use discretion. Often it is simpler to match up wood colours by using dry powder colours with beeswax or paraffin wax.

## Flymarks, to remove
These annoying little black specks will sometimes come away quite easily by just brushing with a hog bristle; at other times they can be really obstinate. If you have a steady hand, try delicately lifting them free with the blade of a scalpel. A judicious little scratch with a fingernail may help. If really firmly fixed, leave a small piece of cotton wool soaked in linseed oil or white spirit on the offending items for about ten minutes and then they should come away without risking damage to the wood surface.

## French polish
This high gloss finish for furniture was developed in the 19th century. The principle is to treat the surface of the wood with shellac dissolved in alcohol, the proportions varying according to the type of wood; if on hardwood a higher proportion of alcohol to shellac is used to produce a thinner consistency. The application is put on with repeated layers until it is felt the gloss achieved is sufficient. The tone and tint can be adjusted by either using different shellacs which can range from pale lemon through to a quite dark orange brown or by dyes added to the alcohol/shellac mixture before it is put on. If French polishing is done well it can leave a rich translucent appearance. Sadly it has often been applied to furniture of the 18th century and even earlier; to do this is to misunderstand the whole feeling of a built-up wax patina. In fact, today some Continental dealers are buying

up good English Georgian furniture, taking it back to their work-shops and stripping it right down, and then giving it the highest gloss French treatment they can. It looks so wrong.

If you do happen upon a good piece of early furniture that has had this atrocious treatment it can generally be rectified but it takes time. Again decide on the value and if it is something good, give it to the professional to deal with. But if just a nice little piece, have a try yourself.

*How to remove it*
There are a number of commercial liquid and jelly paint strip-pers which will serve. *Warning*: As most of these are pretty strong, wear rubber gloves and protect eyes and skin from splashes. The stripper can be applied with a piece of cotton wool or a soft brush. Try to get on as even a coat as possible. Leave for the prescribed time and then swab off with more cotton wool which has been slightly moistened with white spirit; persevere in this way rather than resorting to a scraper which can easily damage the underlying wood. Carving will need a small stiff brush to free all the details of the dissolving polish. When all the old French polish is away, give a thorough rinse with plenty of white spirit. After this has dried right out, repolish with a good beeswax mixture (see *Beeswax polish*).

*How to revive it*
If the piece is of later date and the French polish was put on as a desired finish, rather than one to hide something or to give a false look, it may have become scratched. If the scratches are very shallow they can generally be successfully treated by rub-bing in a little beeswax that has been melted down with a small amount of natural resin. Warm the wax and resin until it can be kneaded with the fingers, then gently massage it into the scratches. If the surface is marred all over by a 'moss' abrasive look, which is probably just the action of time and use, it can be brought back to life by a careful application of this mixture:

3  *parts raw linseed oil*
4  *parts methylated spirits*
2  *parts turpentine or white spirit*
1  *part beeswax*

Shake the wax, methylated spirits and turpentine or white spirit (all three are inflammable) together until the wax has been assimilated and then add the linseed. Apply sparingly with a wad of cotton wool or soft cloth with a gentle circular motion with slight pressure.

## Furniture construction, repairing

The answer here rests entirely on how good is the skill with carpentry and how good is the piece to be operated on. Once you start a major dismemberment with dowels, tenons, dovetails and the rest it can be a big job and really to achieve a good final result does beg for the special skill of a craftsman.

Some damage however can be remedied quite simply. A common occurrence is for a stretcher to the legs of a chair to break; generally this will be more in the nature of a split along the grain. Animal glue or a synthetic adhesive (see PRODUCTS) specifically intended for wood can be used. Apply sparingly to both of the sheared surfaces, let go tacky and bring together. Firm pressure can be applied with a 'G' clamp or by tightly binding with cord (*see diagram 1*). When using clamps with anything, always put

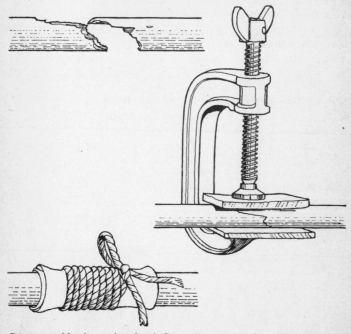

*Diagram 1  Mending a clean break. Be certain to protect the surrounding wood when applying pressure, with small scraps of hardwood when using a 'G' clamp or with stiff fabric under a cord*

something in between the jaws and the material being pressed, otherwise ugly bruising and denting can occur; small pieces of ply or scraps of hardwood will serve. Other fractures to such as legs, arm rests, uprights can be treated in a similar fashion. If the break is an old one and has been botched some years ago, perhaps the two parts have not been put together quite correctly, so loosen the old glue and start again. Place swabs of cotton wool moistened with water around the area and this should after an hour or so soften the earlier glue. Clean off all traces of this before making a fresh start. Remove old glue, also, before repairing a dovetail; reglue and fit together carefully (*see diagram 2*).

If a member has had rather too much attention from a boring beetle, or if there is some trace of old rot it will need consolidation. This can be done by injecting with a proprietary liquid (see PRODUCTS) made for the purpose, or by diluting a selected synthetic glue with acetone and passing this into the damaged wood with a hypodermic. Some craftsmen subject the damage to a thorough soaking with a fairly strong size.

## Gesso and gilding

Furniture decorated with these is prone to damage from knocks. To deal with such mishaps, it is necessary to know that the underlying material, the gesso, is basically a mixture of a plaster and a water soluble glue. In the past master craftsmen have had their secret recipes that have included methods such as using an over-slaked plaster of Paris, *ie* one that has been left standing

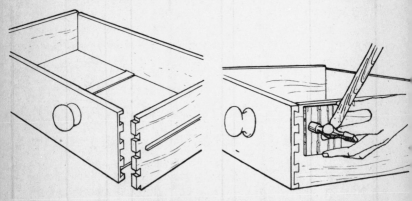

*Diagram 2  When repairing a dovetail, reglue and tap gently with a hammer or mallet, inserting a protective sliver of wood*

with about 5 cm (a couple of inches) of water on top for a fort-
night, when it will have become slaked, mixed with the curds of
milk which has been left to sour for three weeks, carefully
strained sturgeon glue and powdered marble with refined gelatine. If you want to make up a serviceable gesso so that you can
repair cracks and chipped areas, just use whiting or kaolin mixed
with rabbit-skin glue that has been diluted to a size. The consistency to aim for is of a fairly stiff paste that will take modelling.
It is normally best to fill in the crack or build up the chipped area
just a little proud, as this will allow for any shrinkage that may
occur. Leave overnight at least; better still for 48 hours. Then,
with a modelling knife and fine sandpapers, work it down until
completely level with the original.

### Gilding with pastes and liquids

Now comes the nasty bit. What do you do about the gilding?
Here, once more, if the piece is of value, pass it to the trained
man. If not, try your own increasing skill. First the naked gesso
should be given a thin coat of a reddish-brown opaque water
colour (the professional would probably use Armenian bole,
which is a dull red clay). This is because gold leaf is so thin that it
needs an underlying warm tone to bring up its richness. Here we
come to the really tricky part, the gold. There are quite a number
of substitutes around, pastes and liquids in many shades of gold.
Nevertheless their use calls for real discretion. They will probably serve well enough with small areas, but be very circumspect
about applying them over large prominent details or wide
expanses, for they are not going to look right and can stand out
sharply. It is possible, however, once they have dried out that the
'look' can be toned in by brushing over some raw and burnt
umber oil colours that have been diluted with white spirit or oil
painting medium.

### Using gold leaf

If you want to try the real thing, it is a bit on the expensive side
because you will have to buy a complete book of gold leaf with
between 25 and 30 sheets, obtainable from a good art shop. Having taken the plunge, prepare the adhesive; traditionally this has
been glair, a preparation of well-beaten egg white with a little
water. But a mixture of 2 parts water with 1 part acrylic matt
medium will serve. Brush on a little of this, allow a few minutes
to go tacky, then pick up with a soft-hair flat brush the fragment
of gold leaf and lower it into position, stroking it flat. Leave to

harden for a day and a night and burnish up with a piece of agate or with hard smooth plastic.

## Grime, to remove heavy
The kind of greasy-gummy mess that is found on specimens from way-out country sales or those foraged from the dank recesses of a back lane junk emporium is the accretion of years. It is a horrible sticky stuff that just will not move with normal polishes; in fact if they are used in an effort to clean the prize find they will only make it worse.

Mix up the following in a bottle:

*4  parts boiled linseed oil*
*4  parts white vinegar*
*4  parts turpentine (white spirit will work)*
*1  part methylated spirits*
*A few drops ammonia*

Shake vigorously and apply with a piece of cotton wool or a soft brush to get into the crevices. It will not only remove the grime but will also considerably revivify the underlying polish.

## Lacquer
An art that is primarily from the East. Superficially there appears some relation to French polish, but the true Oriental lacquering is a far more refined process. The lacquer comes from *Rhus vernicifera*, the lacquer tree, and after it has been prepared with selected colouring matter is painstakingly applied, up to thirty coats, each being rubbed down when dry before the next is put on. The resultant surface is very hard but also brittle and will crack if the support beneath moves. Hairline cracks can best be filled with a creamy paste of plaster of Paris and shellac dissolved to saturation point in methylated spirits, plus a colouring material. Rub in with a piece of cotton wool. When dry, gently buff up the surface with some potato flour (see WHERE TO GET WHAT) to which has been added a few drops of poppy oil (obtainable from a herbalist or art shop).

## Marquetry
Here problems can come from the fact that there have been many kinds of wood used from different parts of the world; and also other materials such as ivory, mother-of-pearl, and tortoiseshell may have been included. With central heating conditions and humidities discussed previously, trouble can come as

the materials react together. Marquetry should always be dusted and polished with care because minute corners will easily catch in cloths. If an area starts to feel rough to the fingertips it probably means that the small pieces are beginning to loosen. If the object is some superb piece of Dutch work, hand it straightaway to the craftsman. If of lesser stature, try working at a small area at a time; rub in some rabbit-skin glue, or strong size, so that it goes well down in between the little fragments. Then lay a piece of greaseproof paper, which has had the underside slightly smeared with olive or sunflower oil, over the area and rub firmly and smoothly with the back of an old spoon or similar tool. After this, leave it standing under the weight of a flat-iron for 24 hours.

## 'Marriage'

Sometimes it happens that when work is started on some strange find from a shadowy saleroom a rather confused situation becomes uncovered. What at first in a hurried moment appeared as a nice little desk begins to exhibit some odd characteristics: different woods, joints and so on. You've got what the trade calls 'a marriage'. I have heard a dealer eagerly bidding for a square piano, then having got it, describing to a brother-in-the-trade how one end would make the best part of a desk, and the other with a little help could grow into a whatnot. This last brings to mind a strange fellow who liked to collect really big pieces to fill the large rooms in his house. Then he moved to a small-roomed house, but could not bear to part with his fine pieces. Nothing daunted, he took a carpenter's saw, and to my sure knowledge, cut in half a worthy 18th century shop counter with drawers and brass drop handles, a double-sided pedestal desk about 1800, a good veneered late-18th-century wardrobe with inlaid decoration, and then reduced a mid-Victorian whatnot to three occasional tables and the bottom part into what I suppose he would have called a cabinet on castors.

If you have the misfortune to come across one of these sad ones that have been hacked about in some way, the best course is to consult with a friendly craftsman who may be able to rescue something worthwhile; he may even have pieces in his loft that have a close relationship with your acquisition and so will be able to replace the wrong bits and make the rest of it just that much nearer to the original. (See also *Nails and screws*.)

## Metal fittings

Iron or steel hinges, locks or plates, if rusty, should be given attention as soon as possible to prevent pitting. If it can be done conveniently and safely, without disturbing the surrounding material, it may be best to take them off for treatment. Should the rust be light, it will come away with a piece of fine emery cloth and a few drops of light lubricating oil. If heavy, it will first have to be given a lengthy soaking with a proprietary rust remover (see PRODUCTS). The pieces can be left overnight wrapped in rags or cotton wool, soaked with the remover. Next morning rinse off with paraffin or white spirit, dry and apply a very thin coat of lanolin or white wax polish (see PRODUCTS). Lacquering does not seem really to suit iron and steel, giving them an unnatural appearance.

Brass fittings may be cleaned electrochemically (see METALS) or with a proprietary polish. If some spots are obstinate, gently rub in some Tripoli or crocus powder (see GLOSSARY) with a fingertip. When cleaned they may be lacquered. Never resort to a course I have heard about. There was this really rather nice tallboy with brass handles and escutcheons that had taken on a deep tarnish. The first attempt involved the application of strong nitric acid; finding that this was not making much progress, a bold attack was made with coarse sandpaper. Away went the tarnish and also a couple of hundred years of patina, and the resulting finish – scratched and acid-stained.

If escutcheon plates and other metal fittings have to be cleaned in position, please spare a moment to cut out some form of shield for the surrounding wood. This can be from stiff card that is then waxed or fairly thick plastic sheet. Rust remover will stain wood quite badly and metal polishes leave unsightly white stains in the cracks unless the wood is shielded.

## Mother-of-pearl

This and other inlay materials such as bone, coral, shells and small flakes of coloured stone and semi-precious stones often have their effect dimmed by layers of browning wax polish which has accumulated over the years, and indeed some of them, for instance the bone and the shells, can have darkened in themselves. When treating, great care is needed not to get the cleaning materials on to the surrounding wood. Cotton buds make useful applicators. First, use a little of the cleaner described under *Grime*. This should clear off the old wax. Now try a clean cotton bud with some 20 vol. hydrogen peroxide to bleach away remaining stains. If they are recalcitrant, mix up a paste of whiting and hydrogen peroxide, again 20 vol., and gently rub this across the inlays. Rinse off with clean water and dry and polish with a good white wax.

## Nails and screws

Both of these can tell quite a lot about the secret life of some much vaunted pieces. If one comes across a mid-20th-century nail hidden deep in the body of a Tudor coffer, either it is a horrid repair or you have an unwanted 'marriage' on your hands. Unfortunately the head of a nail can be quite craftily disguised by an experienced bit of knocking around to give the Elizabethan look, and then a touch of 5% nitric acid around the edge will produce a convincing rust stain. Screws have also been doctored, and machine-made screws that appear in early Georgian pieces which have not been restored are warnings. Machine-made screws did not appear until 1851.

The butchering that some fine pieces endure in their lives is quite startling. There are buyers who seem to go on the principle that if it looks all right from the front and on top, everything must be fine. In a well-furnished upstairs sitting-room I was admiring an early oak cradle, fine well-polished wood or so it seemed, but removing some cushions I found that three of the bottom boards must have been broken at one time and quite recently they had been replaced with some plain white deal pieces of a packing case with one of them still stencilled with the name of its contents. Worse, they had been fixed down with oversize oval nails with the tops bent over; in several places the oak sides had split under the treatment.

### Removing obstinate nails and screws

Nails and screws that have been used in this way can be very hard to remove without causing further damage. Sometimes a few drops of penetrating oil may help, but if not, try a little local heat. Touch the head of the nail or screw with the tip of a redhot poker. When doing this, it will help to prevent scorching of the surrounding wood if a metal washer is placed round the head being treated and then the poker can be applied through the central hole (*see diagram 3*). If there is still resistance, use more oil and heat. Sadly, with nails, it will nearly always be necessary to sacrifice a small amount of wood to allow pincers to get a grip, but better a well-stopped hole than to leave an unsightly bodging.

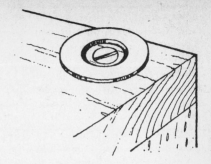

*Diagram 3  Protect surrounding wood before applying a red hot poker to an obstinate screw*

## Ormolu

Bronze or brass gilded ornaments for furniture, also for candelabra and other decorative uses. This often becomes dull and tarnished because the underlying brass or bronze sweats through the gold surface. With care, it can be treated in a number of ways. Where possible it should be dismounted from the piece of furniture. One recipe is to make up this solution:

*1.1 l (2 pints) distilled water*
*25 g (1 oz) sodium hydroxide (caustic soda)*
*75 g (3 oz) sodium potassium tartrate*

Shake well until the chemicals are thoroughly dissolved and then apply with a soft nylon brush. Leave for a few minutes and then rinse well with plenty of clean water. If the piece can only be treated in position, use a stout masking tape to protect the wood.

*Warning*: Wear rubber gloves and avoid splashes on skin or eyes.

Another rather more powerful recipe for obstinate cases is:

*30  parts of 3% nitric acid*
*1   part of alum*

Brush and gently agitate and then thoroughly rinse. Follow the same precautions as above.

If ormolu handles become sticky from use, they may be washed with warm soapy water containing a spoonful of white vinegar. Rinse and then buff up with a soft cloth or chamois. Metal polishes should never be used on ormolu as they will abrade away the gold.

## Parquetry

Inlays of patterns built up with woods of the same colour often over the years darken to the extent that it is hard to appreciate the work. Much of this is multi-layers of polish. This can gener-ally be cleared by using the cleaner previously described under *Grime.* Do a small area first with a cotton bud and then gradually work across the decoration. Try to keep the cleaning even. Sluice away the cleaner with white spirit applied with cotton wool. With care, a further step could be to moisten a piece of cotton wool with a little methylated spirits and gently wipe this over the surface, watching carefully as you go. Again wipe over with white spirit. Give the awakened design a feed with a light application of teak oil and the next day repolish.

## Patina

An all important feature with not only antique furniture but also other materials connected with antiques: bronze, pewter, silver and other metals, stone, leather and painted surfaces. The patina may have been artificially introduced, as with bronze treatments or sculpture. Perhaps most of all it is a subtle something that enrobes a thing of craftsmanship from the past with an almost invisible covering. The mellow gold of long waxed and rubbed oak has a satisfying beauty of its own; the richer, more colourful gleam of fine veneers is precious. In a way they are akin to a glaze that releases to the full the mature quality of fine woods. It is something that should be respected and protected, not savaged away by the brutal use of chemical strippers. Once gone, a patina is almost impossible to replace. Some of the reproduction experts can get close but not enough to take in the true connois-seur who is *simpatico* with the work of the craftsman and the ennobling hand of time.

Whenever working with a cleaner, be careful that it is not of a strength that will carry it through that nearly invisible veil. Try out a small area first.

## Pests

See *Woodworm*

## Polishes and polishing

The choice here as one wanders down the shelves of the iron-monger and hypermarket can bring on a nasty turn of maziness. Row upon row of tins, jars, tubes, pots, aerosols all set to bring up the great polish of all time. There are hard pastes, soft pastes, thick creams, thin creams, liquids and impregnated cloths.

What is required from a polish? That it should do a bit of cleaning and then produce a light-reflecting surface that will help one appreciate more the material it has been applied to; further that it should give a lasting protection. It is helpful as well if it will be resistant to fingermarks and probably pawmarks too, and not have a residual softness that can then be transferred to the clothes of someone who comes in contact with it.

To bring out the real quality of the furniture, what should be aimed for is not a polish that gives an over-bright, glassy glister but rather one that gives a gleam, a sheen that compliments the material underneath but does not obscure it with the startling brilliance it produces. A modicum of muscle power and a length of patience will in general give a more satisfying result. See PRO-DUCTS for suggestions of preparations that will best answer these needs.

As mentioned earlier, it is important to choose the right con-sistency of a polish for a particular job. Solid oak, beech and other woods can be happily brought up with really stiff pastes, whilst veneers and the more delicate inlays will be best served with creams of varying thicknesses. Whatever polish is selected, don't spread it with the 'bread and butter' technique; it is a myth probably fostered by some polish makers that a good thick layer of polish will bring the best result. It should be applied almost sparsely, evenly and over the whole surface so that no areas are missed. The cloth should be soft, and for carved details or mouldings a soft brush may be necessary to get the polish right into the details. Having put the polish on, in many cases it is best to leave it for about 10 or 20 minutes. Then with another soft cloth, which should be inspected to make sure there are no gritty particles on it, start the real job of finding that magic sheen that brings to life your treasure. Work away across the surfaces with a circling motion, again trying to keep an even coverage.

*Once-a-year treatment*

Under the heading of *Grime* a fairly strong recipe was proposed for using with really dirty objects. But in many cases furniture may just have got dirty from household dust, plus the general greasy dirt from the atmosphere. Over the year it may not be practical to spare the time every week or so to give the furniture a thorough cleaning. Polishing will remove much, but there is likely to be a build up of dirt with time. For a special spring cleaning, wash the furniture and then give it a polish. The washing recommended is strictly a two-bucket affair, one with a mixture of warm water and a mild liquid soap (not a soapless detergent) and the other with warm water for rinsing. Wash the wood with a soft cloth or towelling that has been dipped in the soapy mixture and then very well wrung out until almost dry. Now, with another cloth dipped into the plain warm water and again well wrung out, rinse off any residual soap and then with more soft cloths or preferably towelling, which must be dry, go over the whole object and dry every surface thoroughly. Upholstery can be protected by odd pieces of waste fabrics pinned carefully over it during the operation. Change the contents of both buckets as they become soiled, otherwise you may be putting on more dirt than you are taking off.

When the object has dried right off, inspect for any minor surface damage; it is quite possible that the dirt taken off may have been hiding an amount of small surface scratches that now are only too obvious. These may be simply treated with a good wax shoe polish of an appropriate tint; or a proprietary liquid scratch remover (see PRODUCTS) may be applied to the blemishes. When whichever you are using has sufficiently dried out, put on the furniture polish itself in the usual way and you may well be surprised at the excellence of the patina you have created or rediscovered.

**Rushwork**
In the seats of chairs or with items such as peasant matting, rushes are prone to damage by dust, particularly that gritty variety that can be thrown up by traffic in towns. The careful use of a vacuum cleaner is the best way to remove this. If they have become grimed they can be carefully washed. Use the minimum amount of a mixture of mild liquid soap and water and a well wrung out cloth; after that rinse off with cold water to which a little salt has been added. The drying should be accelerated as far as possible. On seats that are somewhat fragile a hair dryer would help. Inspect for woodworm, for although rushwork is not high on their list of preferred foods, they may have had a random bite. If so, a protective application of an appropriate liquid pest preparation (see PRODUCTS) should be made. If the humidity is high, it will do no harm to protect against moulds by using an atomising spray with a saturated solution of thymol in alcohol. (A saturated solution is one in which as much as possible of a solid substance has been dissolved in a liquid.) *Warning*: there is of course a fire risk when spraying alcohol.

## Stain removal

Many substances can be spilt on to furniture; tables generally catch the worst. Most stains will come off without trouble by using a damp cloth if the polished surface is in good state. Some can be more tricky and need special treatment.

### Acids

As soon as possible neutralise by sponging off with a solution of 5 ml (1 level tsp) of borax or washing soda to 600 ml (1 pint) warm water, then rinse with clear water. Old dried-out acid stains should be neutralised and then treated as for *Water and heat* stains.

### Alkalis

Apply a soft rag that has been dipped in an equal part mixture of water and white vinegar. Dried out alkali marks should have the same treatment and then be attended to as for *Water and heat* stains.

### Candle wax

First course should be an attempt to loosen it, as a direct application of white spirit may only semi-dissolve it and smear it into the wax polish that has been applied. Some crushed ice in a piece of muslin can be laid over the wax spillage; this should make it more brittle. After a few minutes, remove the ice and a delicately applied fingernail should shift the offender. Dry, and give a quick buff with a soft cloth with a suspicion of polish on it.

### Ink

If caught whilst still wet, all should be well – just use a damp cloth. But if it has dried right into the surface and maybe even into the underlying wood, this is a nuisance. It will depend on the nature of the ink, the polish and the wood and how long ago it happened. Experiment using small applications with cotton buds and have rinsing liquids at hand. White vinegar is a possible solvent, so is citric acid or lemon juice; a one-to-four solution of 20 vol. hydrogen peroxide may help, or a weak solution of oxalic acid (*warning*: poisonous). On pale stripped woods lemon juice and salt can be the answer. If none of these is a match for the stain, very carefully try a weak solution of household bleach put on with a cotton bud; the strength may be increased as you feel your way through. All these applications should be adequately rinsed away afterwards. If the area is a bit pale after such affronts, and it may well be, judicious treatments with shoe polish or minute quantities of a wood stain will help, followed by a good repolishing.

### Nail varnish remover

A drop or two of this can wreak really nasty damage to a fine old patina. It will quickly penetrate right through to the wood, and the drops have an unpleasant habit of flattening out to cover an area of up to 2–3 cm (1 in) in diameter. First aid, dab it off with anything that is to hand: crumpled newspaper, paper tissue. Then inspect and you may well find that there is a disc-like depression right through the beloved patina on the oak dresser. Your first step now should be to take a wad of cotton wool moistened with white spirit and work over the damage with a circular motion, the idea being to dissolve down the edges of the old polish layers so that after a few minutes it will be a very shallow depression. A few drops of teak oil (see PRODUCTS), perhaps a little colouring from shoe polish and then repolish.

### Oils and grease

Although these are not really much of a menace, if such items as butter, cream, olive oil, and other greasy and fatty substances are allowed to settle for too long they will make the surface smeary and unpleasant. Immediate treatment need be little more than a touch with a cloth and a suspicion of polish. For such stains of senior vintage use a piece of cotton wool and a little white spirit.

### Paints
### Acrylics

If caught whilst still moist these will come away with a rag and water. If dried out they will need the application of a pad of cotton wool moistened with methylated spirits placed over them for probably half an hour. This will not help the patina but neither does a gob of cadmium yellow. With a fingernail or a soft wood spatula ease off the softened colour and treat the area for damaged patina (see *Nail varnish remover*).

*Household emulsion paints* These respond to water whilst wet, but once hardened will need either the same treatment as for the acrylics, or for oils, depending on their type.

*Oil colours* Whilst still soft these will remove readily with a rag and white spirit. If hardened, they may need a few drops of stripper; after about 30 seconds scrape away and repair ravages (see *Nail varnish remover*).

*Tar*

With dry cotton wool wipe off as much as possible, then make applications of eucalyptus oil or turpentine to remove traces. If the tar has been there for a long time, warm it gently first of all and it should respond to the treatment.

*Water and heat*

Here can also be included those wet glass ring-marks that the careless cocktail friend leaves as a visiting reminder on the lid of the grand piano or the best loved pie-crust table. These blemishes can range from the above to quite large areas where someone has rested a kettle, spilt boiling water, placed a scalding platter of soup without a table mat and the rest. All such marks can be annoyingly tenacious. But with perseverance one or other of the recipes below should bring success.

*115 ml (4fl oz) olive oil*
*25 g (1 oz) paraffin wax*

Gently heat together until the wax has melted and blended with the oil. Apply sparingly to the marks, leave for about an hour, rub off and if necessary repeat.

**or**   *4 parts linseed oil*
      *1 part turpentine*

Working out of doors, simmer the linseed oil for 15 minutes, allow to cool and then add the turpentine. Shake before use and apply quite liberally with cotton wool, then leave the soaked pad over the mark for about 12 hours. Wipe off and repolish.

*Warning*: there is a fire risk, which is why it is sensible to work in the open air, and linseed oil also gives off some pretty unpleasant thick smoke during the simmering.

Camphorated oil can often succeed too, as can a paste of olive oil and salt if left overnight. Potato flour (see WHERE TO GET WHAT) and white vinegar can draw out small spot stains.

**Stopping holes etc.**

Often old furniture will have all too many holes where there may have been some attempts at filling or they may have been just left. Usual places are around handles, locks, hinges and escutch-eons. With a little patience these can be largely camouflaged. There are a number of proprietary stoppers (see PRODUCTS) that come in various tints to suit the different woods and there is also the so-called 'plastic wood'. But it is just as simple to prepare your own, using fine sawdust mixed with rabbit-skin glue or a suitable synthetic adhesive to form a paste. This may be tinted with dry powder colours. Working from burnt umber, raw umber, ivory black, burnt sienna and yellow ochre, most woods will be successfully matched. As this and the commercial stoppers are prone to shrink, all holes should be filled proud. After some practice, details that have been damaged with carving, or knot chunks that have gone missing from chair legs can be tackled. Again, see the stoppers are in excess. After they have hardened they can then be worked at with a knife blade and finally abraded to shape, with extra-fine glass-paper and then polished.

## Stripping

Quite often pieces are come across that have been thoughtlessly smothered in one paint or another and it is difficult to be sure as to just what is underneath. There have been many happy finds. Be prepared to work through several layers, as a friend of mine did. He started off thinking it was just a simple case of a small painted pine corner cupboard. The first layer was yellow, the next green, followed by an ugly brown, a white, and more of the brown. As he worked on it, blurred details sharpened. At the finish there was a rather charming oak corner cupboard with brass escutcheon and ribbing.

There are a number of proprietary strippers, both liquid and jelly (see PRODUCTS). They are best put on with an old brush, then when the paint layers start to wrinkle and bubble they can be removed with a stiff scrubber or paint scraper. Be careful if using the latter, as it could easily damage delicate mouldings and other details that might be underneath. Have adequate quantities of white spirit or methylated spirits to sluice away the stripper.

*Warning*: Always wear rubber gloves and watch out to protect the face and eyes from splashes. If you should nevertheless get a splash on bare skin, wash it off immediately with plenty of cold water.

The professionals in the stripping trade will often immerse solid wood pieces in a tank of caustic soda, after which the pieces are neutralised by an immersion in vinegar and water, followed by copious rinsings in plain water. There are definite snags in this treatment. The soda can darken the wood, whereupon the stripper will give the unfortunate wood a strong peroxide bleach. Furthermore the soda takes the natural oils out of the wood, laying up shrinking and cracking for the future. Yet another drawback is that if the soda is not all properly rinsed away the piece will start 'bleeding' and crystalline deposits of soda will appear; if they are wiped away, they will be back. All in all, it is not recommended that amateurs should venture into this field and anyone who decides to do so needs to take considerable care to protect eyes, face and any exposed skin, as stressed previously.

Stripped pine can look pleasant after proper cleansing with just a thorough waxing and polishing; rub in several thin coats of the beeswax polish described earlier. This will give a more harmonious effect than any varnish or synthetic surface treatment.

## Upholstery

Where the upholstery is associated with pieces such as sofas, couches and easy chairs repair can be a highly specialised matter and should certainly be left to an expert. But where it is concerned with chairs with loose seats and padded backs the job can be within reach. The item that most often needs attention is the webbing that is criss-crossed underneath the seat to carry the springs which are tied to the webbing to prevent them from shifting.

### Replacing old webbing

By the time you have removed the hessian or cambric dust-cover underneath the seat and exposed the old webbing there may be a shock at the first glimpse of the seat stretchers – one mass of splintery holes from countless replacement of the webbing straps. Examine for worm; if present, brush over with a liquid killer (see PRODUCTS). If the stretchers are sound the holes can be filled by forcing 'plastic wood' into them with a scraper. Although most people will use iron tacks, copper are really better as there will be little likelihood of rotting from rust in the new webbing.

Old tacks can be a problem to shift and one has to rely on one of those fork-headed lifters. If easing out tacks for replacing the covering of the seats or backs, rest the lifter on a small slip of hardwood or metal to stop bruising where it might show. If the old horse-hair padding has gone out of shape and lumpy, replace it with a good quality high density foam rubber. When fixing the new webbing it is important to get it really tight (*see diagram 4*); if this is not done the springs will move and the seat can become distorted. (See also chapters on TEXTILES and LEATHER.)

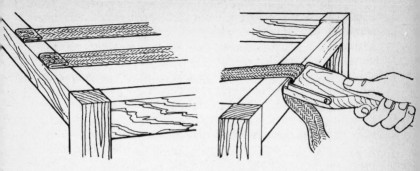

*Diagram 4 Attach webbing to one side of the chair, folding it over twice to give a firm holding for the tacks. Use some form of stretching tool to pull the webbing tight across the frame. Tack twice, cut to length, fold twice and complete tacking as on first side*

## Veneers, repairing
### Chipped veneers
Where small fragments have been knocked off, their loss, even though tiny, often sticks out like the proverbial sore thumb. A do-it-yourself-dealer will often carry stocks of a number of different wood veneers. Persuade him to let you have some small pieces and set yourself up for an afternoon of patient but rewarding effort. A surgeon's scalpel is the best cutting tool; make the cuts with the veneer pieces on a piece of thick but fairly soft cardboard. Use animal glue please (see PRODUCTS), rabbit-skin if possible. Clean off residual muck and using a small paint brush, apply the glue to both surfaces. Allow to go tacky then gently guide the tiny fragments into place and where possible leave under pressure to dry out.

### Cracked veneers
See *Cracks*

### Veneers lifting
This can be caused by a change of environment or by the glue just perishing. Isolated areas of blistering can be caused by spillage of water, or veneer can be sprung because a hot object has been placed upon it. If these bubbles are reasonably small they are best treated as follows: make an incision lengthways with a fine pointed scalpel blade, gently ease the cut open a little way, and with a small brush insert fresh glue, possibly rabbit-skin or

hoof is best, let the cut close, cover with a piece of greased paper and place a flat-iron on top; leave for 24 hours.

If there is a likelihood of accretions of dust and old glue underneath the blister, it may be necessary to cut a flap with the scalpel. This can then be raised and the muck removed; a lens blower as used by photographers will do the job well.

Not infrequently veneer lifts come on curved surfaces; to get these to go down, it will be necessary to cut a former or mould with a curve that will fit where the repair is taking place – use a spare bit of wood for this. It is essential to wedge or bind this in place so that it fits snugly.

If the blisters are small or where there have been corner lifts, a hypodermic syringe can be handy to get the glue into precisely the right place. Some of the synthetic wood adhesives are suitable; polyvinyl acetate, PVA, is convenient to use, and if thought too thick it may be thinned with water. Any spillage is easily wiped away with a damp rag.

Where there is evidence of almost wholesale detachment, leave it to the skilled hand.

**Vernis Martin**
A hard lac varnish which is still more or less the secret of the Monsieur Martin who invented it early in the 18th century. It could be used as a preparation for a wooden panel support for painting; also for treating small wooden objects. It has a resistance to cracking and a hard durable surface. If you come across what you think is a 'Vernis Martin' finish, be careful with any solvents used. Methylated spirits could attack and it is best just to wipe it over with a piece of cotton wool with a touch of white spirit.

**Woodworm**
One of the most insidious attackers of furniture, as well as other timbers in a house, is the grub of this nasty little insect. Investigation comes up with the unpleasant fact that more than 70% of dwellings are offering refuge to this free-loader. Careless husbandry can do much to make these visitors feel at home. As pointed to earlier, the female has a great liking for cracks and corners in woodwork that have been allowed to collect dust and grime. Into this muck she can lay her dozen or so eggs, that in time hatch out the wriggling larvae which then start to gnaw their destructive way into the Chippendale, oak or stripped pine. They will advance along a self-made tunnel just under 1.6 mm ($\frac{1}{16}$in) in

diameter at a speed of around 5 cm (2 in) a year – not all that fast, but more than enough if the rest of the family are at it. The larvae eventually change into pupae which, after two or three years of comfortable hibernation, split open; then out of the tiny tunnel-mouths comes the next generation to carry on the destruction.

The woodworm or furniture beetle unfortunately is not the only member of this boring group. There is the dreaded death watch beetle which can munch holes around 3 mm ($\frac{1}{8}$ in) in diameter through the largest beams, and the wretched thing can have a life cycle of up to ten years or more, a first class 'sleeper' if ever there was one. After him, or her, come the longhorn beetle, a fast driller that originated on the Continent, and the powder post beetle which has a liking for the softer woods. Other materials these predators appreciate include basketwork, papier mâché, paper, cardboards, rushes and bamboos. One of their real treats is a softwood three-ply sheet, such as is all too often put behind mirrors and pictures – replace with hardboard as soon as possible!

*How to deal with pests*
Follow up the earlier advice about inspection. First, are there any signs of active drilling, evidenced by tiny piles of wood-powder near suspected targets? Generally these tunnellers like to make a start in the shade, at the back of, or underneath, the object selected. If there are drill holes, do they look fresh? If the infestation is slight it can be dealt with by using one or other of the proprietary liquids (see PRODUCTS). These come in aerosols and containers that can be squeezed.

*Warning:* when making any application it is essential to have plenty of ventilation. Do not let the liquid contact the skin, wear rubber gloves, and certainly keep it well away from the eyes; it is wise to wear some kind of protection, glasses or goggles, as the ramifications of the little tunnels can sometimes reach quite a way. What can happen is that you squirt into one hole and then unexpectedly a jet will issue perhaps some 15 cm (6 in) away.

After treatment lasting protection for the wood can be to use every now and then a polish that contains an anti-woodworm ingredient.

If there is evidence of sporadic infestation around a room, this can often be discouraged by the use of a fumigating device with a wick which is obtainable from a good ironmonger. Shut the windows, light the wick and retire shutting the door. Once lit it pours out a dense white cloud that will gradually envelop the whole room, which should be left shut up for 48 hours. But if the attack is wholesale, reach for the phone and call in a firm offering eradication service.

# Ceramics

Here come some of the more lovely objects we collect but also they are among the most fragile. When one notes the rate of chipping, cracking and smashing that goes on today with general use, it seems amazing the number of these beautiful wares that have survived all those many years of handlings, removals and other dangers, man-made and natural. If dealing with worthwhile pieces, give them the gentle care they need. When stacking quality plates on top of one another, put a few sheets of paper in between each to ease possible abrasive action. Don't lift those precious Meissen cups just by the handles and furthermore don't stack them one inside another. All very elementary but sometimes overlooked and then frail decoration can become damaged. Leave space around dishes and plates in the cupboard: it does not take much of a knock for a shell chip.

## Wares and techniques

*Biscuit*
Earthenware or porcelain that has had a first firing, before it has been glazed. It is also called *bisque*. As with other unglazed ware, cleansing should be minimal; if possible just by dusting with a soft-hair brush or wiping with moistened cotton wool. A little mild soap or a few drops of detergent may be added. Afterwards apply several swabs with just water.

*Bone china*
A patent for manufacture was taken out in 1748 by Thomas Frye of Bow. A mixing of bone ash or calcium phosphate with china clay.

## Crackle

A glaze that is purposely applied in a certain way so that it will end up with a fine network of cracks. It is also called alligator glaze. If building up a small or large repair to a piece with this glaze it poses a tricky problem. If an attempt is made to simulate the cracks by a surface application it is unlikely to succeed. It is better to work on the repair after it has set and been painted. Use either a medium hard pencil or some sepia ink to which a few drops of black ink have been added; apply this with a fine mapping pen. Don't hurry, and keep looking at the crackle around the repair so that you can simulate the effect. Before putting on the cold setting glaze (see *Glaze substitute* on page 54) give just a short spray with some fixative which will help to hold ink and, particularly, pencil in place.

## Earthenware

Vessels made from a coarser fired clay, possibly a mixture of ball clay, china clay, ground stone and ground flint. Although it might appear to be strong, it has little resistance to chipping and under the glaze is porous.

## Encaustic tiles

Those that are decorated with inlaid clays and then fired. In 1769 Josiah Wedgwood took out a patent for a process very close to this method.

## Faïence

A rather broad term that today takes in most kinds of white pottery. Earlier this denoted a decorative earthenware with a tin glaze, the name being derived from Faenza in Italy. Faïence and pottery should not be completely immersed in water when cleaning; they should be gently wiped over with a cloth that is slightly damp. If grime is obstinate, a few drops of a gentle detergent can be added to the water the cloth is dipped in. Where faïence pieces have metal mounts, these should be cleaned in ways suggested in METALS.

## Flash

A term for a firing malfunction, it is when pottery becomes discoloured because of being in direct contact with the flames. Therefore if you spot such a condition, don't try to remove same

## Frit

A compound of certain materials that are partly or wholly fused and put to use as a basis for certain glazes. It can contain alkalis, boric acid, lime, silica and sometimes lead oxide. Frit may also be a semi-fused stony mass of similar materials that is used to give a certain density to soft-paste porcelain.

## Glaze

Vitreous coating for porcelain or pottery, it may be transparent or opaque. Lead, tin and salt are among the better known varieties.

## Hard-paste

Porcelain manufactured from kaolin (China clay) and petuntse (feldspar or China stone, in England also known as Cornish stone). The latter gives a translucence.

## Soft-paste

Porcelain that is made mostly from bone ash and gypsum by European potters in an attempt to rival or imitate the Eastern hard-pastes. It is fired at a low temperature and made translucent by a previously fired glassy mixture.

## Stoneware

Coarse potter's ware glazed and fired to density at temperatures up to 1400° Centigrade.

## Terracotta

A material of brownish-red clay that is fired but generally not glazed. If the craftsman does his job correctly it can have considerable permanence. It was much used for modelling small figures and decorative groups, also decorative ornaments for buildings. There are examples that have been glazed and also some that have been painted. The figurines from Tanagra in Greece, dating from Classical times, are good examples of early work, although sadly they have been much faked. To clean, the first step should be to dust carefully with a soft-hair brush. A little whiting can be worked into details to bring away accumulated grime. If this does not succeed, a little water with a few drops of gentle detergent may be brushed over the piece, followed by brushing with clean water and a thorough drying with cotton wool and soft cloths. Some give a protective coat of a fine white wax polish, but use the minimum or the appearance will be too drastically altered.

*Unfired antiquities*
These should never be brought into contact with water. The only course is to give them a very careful light dusting with a soft-hair brush.

## Problems, products and processes

Experimenting with the first simple steps of ceramic care can be fascinating, and will encourage more ambitious practices. Here are some of the materials to use and methods to try.

### Adhesives
Fifty years ago the china mender still had mainly to rely on the traditional glues made from shellac, animal and fish substances, all of them dark in tone and liable to go darker. Here the chemist has helped greatly with a range of single-tube, water-clear synthetic adhesives and those synthetic types that come in twin packs, the glue and the hardener (see PRODUCTS). These epoxy glues have a slight but acceptable opacity and tint.

*'Instant' glues*
Of the single tube varieties the 'instant' glues can be very useful, particularly for small mends. It seems too that they will stand up well against handling afterwards and also washing up; indeed I have found a handle on a non-vintage cup that had been re-affixed with this substance withstood the hustle and bustle of a washing-up machine for over a year.

*Warning*: When the manufacturers call these glues instant they really mean it, so be prepared. When setting a join, have everything ready and be exact with the placing. Watch for spillages and clean up at once. Acetone can help if there are traces of unwanted dried out bits. A further word of caution: these 'instants' stick just about everything to everything and this includes you to you, you to china and you to the work bench. If there is an undesired attachment, it should be treated with hot water and patience. Don't try and force the stuck fast fixed finger and thumb apart.

*Two-tube glues*
These glues have been so tailored by the manufacturers that there is now practically a specialised epoxy glue for every need,

although most of them still work with groups of like surfaces. Have a rout round the hardware shop and choose those that seem most in line with your problem. They all work on the same principle of squeezing out equal portions of the glue and hardener. It is best to mix on a piece of scrap glass with a palette knife. Don't make up too much, for as soon as the mixing starts, so does a chemical reaction which begins the setting process. At first the mix is a sticky viscous liquid, then after about 15 minutes it starts to stiffen and within an hour it is near to solid. Epoxy glues will give a firm set within 12 hours but if left for a week will come up with a rock-firm fix. If in a hurry, gentle heat from a lamp bulb or an airing cupboard will give a firm joint in about three hours.

There is one slight but acceptable disadvantage with the epoxies and instants. This is that they are very nearly irreversible; at early stages acetone will stop the setting, but once set, about the only course I have found that works is a long immersion in hot water with rather too much detergent in it for the comfort of elderly pieces. Therefore get everything ready before making a start, so that when the break has been repaired it has been done absolutely right the first time.

*Warning*: It is advisable to have adequate ventilation when working with any of the synthetic glues, as the odours given off can be upsetting. Try to keep them off the hands as far as possible.

## Breaks

The single fragment or break into two main pieces with one join line should give little trouble. If it has just happened the edges will not need cleaning. Put the chosen adhesive, either epoxy or instant, on both surfaces to be joined, spreading out as thinly as you can with the scalpel. It is important that as little glue is used as possible, so as to achieve the desired hair-line join. Bring the two pieces together with firm pressure and then tape tightly with Sellotape or gummed strips. Now lay the object to rest in a ready prepared bed. This may be of Plasticine, or sawdust covered with a piece of tissue paper or any device to take the weight off the parts whilst the glue is setting. After 24 hours, examine and remove any signs of excess glue, shaving off with the scalpel.

### Multi-breaks

Never try to stick all the pieces together at the same session. Pick on the largest fragment and start working outwards with pieces that actually touch this most substantial fragment. Here again it is more vital than ever not to put on too much glue as even a slight over-thickness will mean that the pieces will not fit quite snugly, and worse, this lack of exact fit is liable to multiply as you work across the repair. Again tape tightly and lay in a supporting bed. Finally, remove excess glue when thoroughly dry.

Treat items such as cup or mug handles in the same basic way. A lump of Plasticine makes a good support to hold the cup so that the re-attached handle stands upright whilst setting (*see diagram 5*).

*Old breaks*
If these have been repaired for some fifty years or more, it is likely that animal, fish or shellac glues were used. By now they can look pretty dismal. Depending on circumstances, aesthetically it would seem that it is preferable to redo the repair. Normally if the piece is put in hot water for about an hour it will come apart. If not, it will not hurt to leave it in longer. But if still obstinate after a night's soaking other ways will have to be tried. A first attempt can be to cover old joins with swabs of cotton wool soaked in methylated spirits. Secondly, try swabs of cotton wool soaked in acetone (*warning*: with this method very adequate ventilation will be needed).

Once having got the fragments separated, clean the edges with a little detergent and water and a small stiff brush. Then try bleaching out any remaining stains. Rebuild as suggested.

*Diagram 5  Moist clay or Plasticine supports a cup whilst its handle is setting*

## Shell breaks

Annoying little flakes knocked off the edges of plates and the like through careless handling. The procedure is to cleanse with detergent and water and degrease with methylated spirits. Prepare some modelling paste (see *Pastes*) and knead this into position and shape, leaving it slightly proud. Two or three hours after, when the paste is stiffening, work at it with a scalpel to bring close to the desired shape. After two or three days, when it is quite hard, bring down exactly to form with fine sandpaper or wet and dry paper. Retouch and apply cool glaze (see *Glaze substitutes*).

## Cracked, but not broken

Often one of the trickiest problems with those best pieces in the china cupboard. If they are just tiny hair cracks and the object is for viewing and not use, leave it. The small cracks are ugly, especially as they tend to gather microscopic accumulations of grime, but it is not worth the risk of taking any remedial steps other than perhaps some applications of a mild bleach with a cotton bud. This can sometimes greatly reduce the evidence of the crack; be certain to rinse the bleach off thoroughly.

### Cleaning a long, grubby crack

If, however, there is that large ironstone or other ware platter that has a grimy crack which goes about two thirds of the way across, as shown in the top diagram *6a* what do you do then? Do you take courage, don a pair of thick leather gloves and force the break right across so that a full-scale mend and cleaning up can be done? There is one other way that will often work. Even a seeming rock-firm material like fired clay can still have a slight elasticity. By the way a third hand will be needed here. Take a firm hold each side of the crack and then with gently controlled strength pull ever so slightly apart. Just as soon as a minute opening appears call to the third hand to slip a pin into the gap fairly close to the edge of the platter (*see diagram 6b*).

Quite a bit of cleaning up can now be done with methylated spirits applied with a very small brush (*see diagram 6c*). When that is dry, brush along the edges with some bleach, leave for about ten minutes and then rinse. The platter should then be left at least overnight, preferably in a little warmth so that it can completely dry out. Finally, ease some of the instant glue into the crack, pull out the pin, and to help matters, tape the joint in several places (*see diagram 6d*); wipe off any spilt glue.

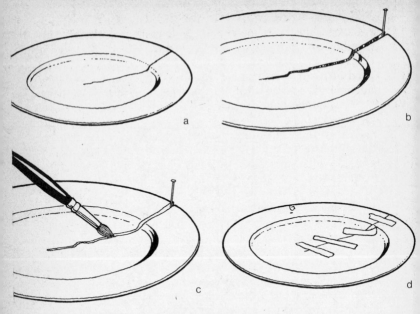

*Diagram 6a, b, c, d Cleaning and cementing a long crack in a plate*

## Fakes
See *Restored for deception*

## Glaze substitutes
Although there is nothing that will replace the hard shine of a fired potter's glaze, there are some products around that will approach it. Varnishes similar to those for paintings can serve for small areas and probably will not be noticed when the piece is back in the display cabinet. But for more general handling there is a good artificial glaze (see WHERE TO GET WHAT) made by a manufacturer in Florence. This is water-clear and will dry out on all ceramic surfaces, and retouches, leaving after about 48 hours, a hard skin that is pretty well proof against a scratching nail. Acetone will dissolve it off if anything goes wrong, but a fairly stiff brush will be needed as the liquid is heavy; thankfully, it is also self-levelling, so brush strokes should not show.

## Gilding, touching up
There is no way of cheating an experienced eye with a high-powered magnifying glass with this one. But what materials are

available can be coaxed into doing a fair deception. In FURNITURE, on page 29, a method for touching up gilt gesso was described, and it is possible to adapt this for china; but a simpler way is to buy one of the ready-mixed artificial golds, either in liquid or paste form, that are obtainable from an art shop. As with applying real gold leaf, it is advisable to give an underlying coat of a warm reddish brown, because this will assist in throwing up a feeling of richness. The commercial golds come in a number of tints and tones that will enable you to match the example being worked on. It is possible to buy varying shades of bronze powders imitating gold; these are also obtainable from an art shop and can be mixed with a varnish before use.

Some wares are decorated with tiny spots of gilding that are slightly raised. To simulate these the liquid golds or those made up from dry powders with varnish will have to have a small amount of kaolin mixed with them to make the mixture 'short' so that it will stand up satisfactorily.

## Modelling a replacement

Here is one of the most fascinating tests for skill; don't shy off and say to yourself it's impossible. Experiment with small items. Most replacements fail because of the lack of preparation. Be quite sure that the areas of attachment are clean. Degrease thoroughly with a cotton bud dipped in methylated spirits. Have whatever paste you have chosen (see *Pastes*, page 58) kneaded to just the right consistency. If the missing part is fairly large, an armature of wire may be needed; an armature is an internal supportive framework. For some pieces, if the main body is sturdy, a tiny hole can be drilled and a small steel support-pin inserted (*see diagram 7a*).

Tiny things like fingers on the hands of figures which are so often the first victims, can be rolled around on the palm of the hand or a small sheet of glass, being trimmed to shape with a scalpel. A touch of adhesive and then adjust whatever has been arranged to support the mend whilst it is drying out. If items like leaves or flower petals are to be fitted, the paste can be first rolled out flat to the desired thickness, then the design can be lightly pencilled or scratched into the surface (*see diagram 7b*). With the sharpest pointed scalpel blade the delicate leaf or petal can be cut out exactly to shape, and necessary folds or curves eased into position with the fingers or by bending the cut out shape over a brush handle (*see diagram 7c*).

After the repair has been in position for two or three hours it

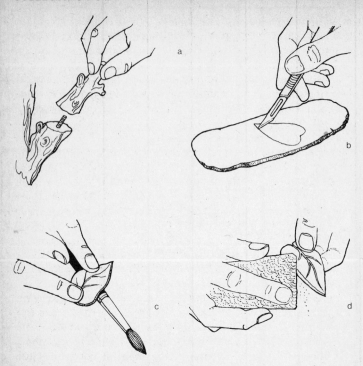

*Diagram 7a A steel support pin helps to hold two pieces firmly together*
*b A replacement petal can be cut out of paste*
*c Use a paint brush handle to shape the replacement*
*d Final adjustments with sandpaper*

will have stiffened up considerably and if adjustments are needed they can be made with the scalpel. Leave for a full two days and the paste will have hardened and so will allow for any further refining by sandpaper or wet and dry paper (*see diagram 7d*).

## Paints for retouching

The choice here is between artist's quality oil colours or a newly introduced type of paint called alkyds, also obtainable from an art shop. For many years restorers have relied on oil colours, which can serve well, but some of the colours can have a lengthy drying time. The alkyd colours have three advantages: the whole range dries out quite quickly and all of them at the same rate and there is very little tonal change between wet and dry. The last point is helpful when retouching, as with some oil colours it can be tricky to judge exactly how the dried-out colour will look.

If either the alkyds or the oils need diluting, this may be done with white spirit; if they require stiffening for impasto touches (see GLOSSARY), small quantities of kaolin, marble dust or whiting may be mixed in with them. For marble dust see WHERE TO GET WHAT.

Discipline is called for with retouching. Put the rays of an ultra-violet lamp on some mangled repair job and the fluorescence will quickly show how clumsily it has been done; areas of retouching have gone way beyond the actual repair. The idiot has hoped to disguise his lack of talent by taking the retouching far over the surface on each side or around the repair.

*The retoucher's palette*
Be patient with this retouching business. Practise mixing the colours and applying them to scrap pieces of broken earthenware so that you get the feel of the matter.

A useful palette or collection of colours to make a start from are: titanium white, cadmium yellow, yellow ochre, cadmium red, light red, Indian red, alizarin crimson, burnt sienna, burnt umber, ivory black, French ultramarine, monastral blue, viridian and terre verte. Only the smallest tubes need be bought because the amounts used will be little.

By far the most difficult colour to match is white. If you think this is a wild statement put a stroke of titanium white on to an area of what you feel is white glaze. It will later be discovered that pretty well all the basic white glazes on the different wares are just that bit off dead white. Get to know them and to be able to judge which of the other colours it is necessary to add: touches of blue, yellow ochre, light red or burnt umber. The whole business is surprisingly subtle. Spare a few hours to work this problem out; it will be time more than well spent and save much frustration later on.

Other mixes should be experimented with so that an intimate working association is established with the palette. A wide variety of greens can come from putting the yellows or the blues with the viridian and terre verte, and of course the yellows with the blues. One often unsuspected source for a green is to mix cadmium yellow with ivory black. Flesh can be a trouble; small touches of French ultramarine, yellow ochre and cadmium red with the white should bring results. Purple and violet tints are best approached by mixing alizarin crimson with one of the blues.

Always do the retouching by daylight, as artificial light can have some strange effects on paints, the blues noticeably being affected. It is worth spending a bit extra to get good brushes. These should be of sable and round in shape (sizes ranging down from possibly a number five to the smallest, the triple goose, which is marked on its handle with ooo). Look after them, rinsing out thoroughly with white spirit after each painting session. Keep them standing upright in a jar and if they are to be stored away, have some anti-moth preparation at the ready as the clothes member of this tribe is particularly fond of good quality sable hair.

### Pastes

These are the basic materials for modelling and filling. There are a number of proprietary brands (see WHERE TO GET WHAT) that are adequate. The better ones consist of two tins of different pastes. An equal amount from each is taken and kneaded together and the paste is ready for use. Your own modelling paste can be made simply by mixing with the ready stirred epoxy glue a little kaolin, marble dust (see WHERE TO GET WHAT) or whiting. The instant glues are not suitable for paste making.

### Plasticine

Have a pound or two around because it can be useful for holding pieces whilst they are setting. It can also serve to make simple moulds if using very soft pastes.

### Restored for deception

It will not be unusual if amongst some newly acquired objects you come across a fake. There is still quite a flow of wrong stuff about and one ruse the rascals use for the issuing of bad ones is, having made the fake, to break it and then restore it, leaving the repairs not over-disguised. For many, the sight of restoration work on an object seems to be a guarantee of authenticity.

### Retouching See *Paints*

### Rivets, replacing

In the days before such adhesives as the epoxies, and where there was a pretty massive break, the repairer used to resort to holding the pieces together with small, flat staple-shaped brass rivets. In most cases, from the appearance point of view, it is now better to replace the rivets. Soak the object as recommended under *Breaks*. If after this the rivets will not come away, they should be eased out with the tip of a knife blade or a small screwdriver. Clean up the object, bleach, reassemble and fill the holes where the rivets were with paste, retouch and cool glaze (see *Glaze substitutes*).

## Solvents
*Alcohol*
This will act on most epoxy glues. Methylated spirits is an easily obtainable form of alcohol.

*Acetone*
This will remove epoxies and also most 'instants'.
   *Warning*: acetone is highly inflammable and the fumes are also toxic, so that it should only be used with very adequate ventilation.

*White spirit*
Useful for cleaning up after using alkyd or oil colours.

## Stain removal
Fortunately, by the nature of most ceramics, they are fairly resistant to staining. Owing to the lack of porosity with the glazes of most wares there is little chance of serious discoloration other than with tea and coffee pots. If the glaze is sound both of these can be cleared with a fairly strong borax solution followed by a mild bleach. Use 50 g (2 oz) borax to 600 ml (1 pint) water. Copious rinsing should be given. With 18th-century pots the bleach should be very weak as it could damage the glaze. A bottle brush will help to dislodge the marks after they have been soaked. Rinse adequately afterwards.
   If pots and other objects with enclosed space are put away wet, it may be found that there are signs of mildew and moulds after a period. These may leave grey-brown staining that should answer to a light bleaching. If the pieces are not to be used domestically, a wipe over with a saturated solution of thymol in alcohol should discourage further trouble.

## Washing the china
The pieces in your collection may be from many sources and from different periods; they can have varied glazes and be in conditions of well-being or not so well-being. Washing the

crocks may seem an easy task, but it needs a little thought and lots of care when dealing with objects of worth. Broadly speaking, an automatic dishwasher is no place for the Sèvres or the Ming. Firstly, some of these labour saving devices can generate a pretty high temperature and secondly, some of the washing powders put out with them could do strange and probably irreversible things to glazes which may be ancient and probably fragile.

Always carefully examine a new purchase from an auction before putting it anywhere near water. Look for glaze trouble and also signs of earlier restorations. If all seems well the safe procedure is to take one piece at a time.

Have a plastic bowl filled with water no hotter than is quite comfortable for the hands. Into this put a few drops of a gentle liquid soap or a good quality detergent. As an extra safeguard, put a sheet of plastic foam about an inch thick at the bottom of the bowl. Then lower the first piece in and gently caress it with a soft cloth, or if there is some complicated detail a soft long-haired brush. Have a second bowl beside you with warm water, and when you are satisfied that the piece is as clean as it is going to come, take it out and carefully swirl it around in the clean water. After this dry it with soft towelling or an absorbent soft linen cloth.

If some objects have a firm glaze and have some thick, greasy marks that are resisting normal washing, these may have a little soap worked into the spots with a brush before going into the water. If that fails, try gently rubbing with a cotton bud dipped in white spirit or methylated spirits, or a piece of spongy substance such as putty that will pick off the grime.

# Glass

Seemingly one of the hardest and most impervious of materials, glass is certainly brittle but has otherwise been protected by its nature from many of the risks that lay in wait for other antique objects. An accident can happen, and here, it is one of the few materials where one is unable to hide a break that has been repaired. Apart from this there is really just one danger to protect glass from and this is damp. The older the glass the more it can be affected.

It is a material of some antiquity; records are not certain about the exact date when it was first made in ancient Egypt, but they do make clear that from the beginning of the 18th Dynasty, around the 16th century BC, there was a regular and quite considerable production. Then, in the way of such things, it faded, and by the beginning of the 10th century BC, the production had nearly stopped. The flame of skilled manufacturing was thereupon to pass to the Romans. But these early glasses differ from those which were to come later. Up to the 17th century almost all glass was composed of silica, lime, and soda or potash. Pliny the Elder, the great relator of strange things, writing in the 1st century AD, left behind a note on the discovery of glass. It is somewhat in the vein of another legend that relates how pottery was discovered by the basket burning with the clay in it. Pliny's glass revelation tells of how a ship laden with natron (a whitish or yellow mineral that consists of hydrated sodium carbonate and is found in saline deposits and salt lakes) was moored somewhere on the sandy shore of Phoenicia and the merchants off the ship were preparing a meal; not finding any stones to support their cauldron they used some lumps of natron from the ship's hold, and the heat of the fire made the natron combine with the sand and so made glass.

Some 16 centuries later it was George Ravenscroft (1618–81) who with the backing of the Glass Sellers' Company set up a glasshouse in the Savoy in London and in 1673 was granted a patent for his formula for 'flint glass' which contained lead oxide. This new glass was stronger, more brilliant when cut and more usable for engraving.

Glass is mainly associated with drinking vessels and liquid containers, but it is also of course used for lighting fittings, mirrors, certain mosaics, stained glass and windows. It has been painted on, back painted on, stained, enamelled, gilded, engraved and acid etched.

# Special problems and techniques

### Acid attack
Certainly the later glasses from Ravenscroft's time are more or less immune to the effects of all the better known acids; in fact two of the acids in dilute states are useful cleaners (see *Stain removal*). Hydrofluoric acid, however, will penetrate the hardness and it has been used for decoration by some craftsmen. First a wax and resin ground is melted and laid on the surface of the glass and into this the design is needled, in the same manner as that for making an etching. Then the hydrofluoric acid is applied and eats into the glass through the marks of the needle which has cut through the ground. Less reputable craftsmen have also taken advantage of this acid and technique to alter signatures and symbols from celebrated glasshouses.

### Adhesives
There are several epoxy two-tube glues on the market which are especially intended for glass, and a word to the manager of a hardware store should produce the right one. The 'instants' mentioned in the previous chapter may be used, and in some ways by their more fluid consistency they can make for a thinner join line. There is also a special instant for glass that relies on ultra-violet rays to bring the set. A recipe for making your own adhesive is as follows:

*195 ml (7 fl oz) ethylene dichloride*
*5 ml (0.17 fl oz) glacial acetic acid*
*Fragments of Perspex*

Mix the first two together and dissolve the Perspex fragments in the liquid. Cork tightly when not being used. Another home-made adhesive for glass is an acid water soluble glue:

*30 ml (1 fl oz) glacial acetic acid*
*20 g (3/4 oz) Scotch or rabbit-skin glue*
*1 g (trace) ammonium bichromate*

Warm the acetic acid and dissolve the two other ingredients in it. Heat up before use in the same way as for using ordinary animal glues.

## Breaks

The strength and adaptability of these modern glues allow for mends that would hardly have been possible fifty or so years ago. With an epoxy or an instant it is quite possible to repair satisfactorily the slender stem of a wine glass that has snapped. As with porcelain repairing put on the minimum amount of the chosen glue to both surfaces to be joined, bring accurately together and then tape tightly and provide adequate support so that there is no tension on the join. Then have possibly even more patience than with porcelain. Leave it to season thoroughly, to harden right out for three or four days at least.

### Replacing a lost fragment

One of the snags about a glass break is that whether it is a small drinking vessel or a large bowl, some of the fragments that splinter away can be very small indeed; in fact they may never be found, so that the repairer can be left at the end of his rebuilding the brittle form with some annoying little holes. It is possible to achieve a reasonable solution with the following procedure.

Stick a piece of Sellotape inside the glass over the back of a hole. Now bed the glass down in a chunk of Plasticine so that the hole being treated is at the top of the glass. With a sharp pointed instrument similar to a dental probe let a droplet of one of the single tube, water-clear, synthetic adhesives fall gently into the small hole, followed by another drop and as much as is necessary to level up to the surface. When the adhesive has hardened, the Sellotape can be pulled away carefully. If dealing with coloured glass, the adhesive could be tinted with small quantities of dyes or transparent pigments before application.

## Chandeliers

These rely on sparkling, pristine cleanliness for the full effect of glorious light. Today many of them will not be the problem they were, as electric bulbs simulate the candles, often hundreds of them, that formerly lit these masterworks of the glass craftsman.

There is one snag with modern fitted chandeliers: in general they are firm fixtures to the ceilings, whereas the earlier ones nearly always had some kind of winch or block and tackle for lowering them for the arduous business of lighting all those wicks. But it did mean that all the beautifully cut glass pendants and drops could be got at for cleaning. The grime would have been mostly from tallow smoke, now it is whatever is brewed up by the environment, but it is still some greasy muck. The implications of cleaning something like this, with literally hundreds of bits, is enough to put to flight the most dedicated paid hand, so the job will probably fall to the owner. This mess can be cleaned off in a number of ways:

1 Hot water with a little detergent and a few drops of ammonia; wear gloves with this.

2 Hot water with a little methylated spirits and white vinegar.

3 One of the proprietary glass cleaners preferably one that comes in a spray applicator.

Whichever one is selected, start at the top and work downwards.

### Drying glass

The most important matter with any type of glass, but particularly so with the older ones, is that it must be absolutely and thoroughly dried even when just being put away overnight in a ready-for-use cupboard. Moisture left in vessels, or on them, or present in the storage place will certainly bring on a cloudiness with the pre-17th-century glasses and it can affect the later ones, even if it only takes off that peak sparkle that is the pride of Waterford and other glasshouses around the map. The likes of decanters have driven many up a nearby wall with efforts to dry them out. There have been dark tales of in-between maids giving them a 'warm up' in the oven when the butler has turned away. There is no really efficient method of getting a cloth down that narrow neck in sufficient quantities to do the job. But a few minutes with a hair dryer and it is done.

For glass in general, a soft linen cloth or a soft chamois are best for drying. Cotton or woollen cloths are of little use as they leave specks of fluff behind. A few drops of methylated spirits can bring up a lustre to the outside of decanters and other vessels, but this must only be used on the outside, never on the inside if the vessels are for domestic use. (Washing is dealt with under this heading on page 68.)

## Enamelled and gilt glass

To really appreciate these highly skilled works they need to be sparkling clean. With a soft chamois lightly moistened with methylated spirits, give them a gentle wiping; after that, another dry chamois and an equally gentle buffing up, the last strokes being more in the way of caresses.

## Engraved glass

Under some conditions the details of the engraving can become semiclogged with greasy dust. This may simply be removed with a soft-hair brush; if obstinate dip the brush in a little methylated spirits.

## Glass stoppers, to loosen

Liable to be tiresome if a decanter has been put away for some time, and the last time it was used the stopper was put in with the neck wet from wine. It is risky to try the often used method of tapping round the edge of the top lip; better to drop a little olive oil so that it runs round the neck and will gradually seep in between the stopper and the neck. Another mixture that can be tried is 2 parts methylated spirits, 1 part glycerine and 1 part salt.

## Iridescence

Often a feature with the very ancient glasses, and it is a sign of deterioration; the more brilliant the iridescence the more the partial decomposition will have advanced. Depending on the particular case, the glass can be thoroughly soaked in distilled water, changing same several times, and then may have an application of a clear varnish to consolidate matters.

Trying to simulate this pearly lustrous look of iridescence is a favourite ploy with the repro-fake fraternity. They go in for such simple ways as sticking fish scales on the inside of the glass or burying the article in manure. One fellow in this category went to a lot of trouble to re-create, as he thought, a piece of early medieval glass, which did not come up too badly except for one small point: he had not noticed that the bottom of the object he was fiddling bore in clear letters a date for this century and the name of a Cork, Ireland glasshouse.

## Metal mounts

Treatments will be suggested in the next chapter, METALS.

## Mirrors

If the silvering has started to deteriorate, do not be tempted to play around with some crackpot recipe to remedy matters. The original glass as it is is precious. When cleaning the front of the mirror it is very important not to let any moisture get behind as this can cause further trouble. The glass can be cleaned with a cloth dampened with methylated spirits. Another method is to put a little ammonia in a bowl of lukewarm water, and wipe over the glass with a cloth that has been immersed in this and then well wrung out. Some traditional ladies still lean on the old one of a little paraffin on a rag; it may be smelly, but it does work.

## Scratches, removing

Moss scratches from overmuch handling can mar an appearance on a bowl or other object. They can be worked away at with a soft chamois dipped in a small amount of jeweller's rouge; use a certain amount of firm pressure with a circular motion, not directional or this may show afterwards. If desired the rouge can be made into a thin paste first with methylated spirits. Scratches under the base should be left: they are a natural result of use (*see diagram 8*).

## Stained glass

In some areas this lovely glass that is the token of the skill and imagination of long past craftsmen is suffering the worst attack in its history. For example, the glass in Canterbury Cathedral that

*Diagram 8 Moss scratching on the base of a glass object can be proof of age. Examination with a magnifying glass may show it has been falsely added*

has withstood the elements for some seven centuries and two wars is now being assaulted by our man-made pollution filled atmosphere. The 12th-century potash glass is beginning to surrender to industrial fumes combined with its old enemy, damp.

If deterioration has advanced as far as it has in Canterbury, it can only be halted and treated by experts. But if stained glass in a house or collection does become over-grimed it may be washed with warm water to which a little ammonia has been added; this may be applied with a soft scrubbing brush which can be used to dislodge the mess gently. Rinse afterwards, and dry thoroughly.

In high humidity areas, mould growths may be noticed and these can also be treated with ammonia and water. Then wipe over with a piece of cotton wool moistened with a saturated solution of thymol in methylated spirits, ie, as much thymol as will dissolve in the quantity of methylated spirits being used.

## Stain removal

Decanters or other vessels that have held liquids that leave a residue are most likely to be affected. There are several recipes for clearing this trouble, including:

1 Pour in about 2–3 cm (1 in) of white vinegar, add 5 ml (1 tsp) of mild scouring powder, nearly fill with warm water, give a thorough shaking and leave overnight; empty and rinse.

2 Pour in white vinegar, add about 10 ml (2 tsp) salt, shake and leave for several hours, then rinse.

3 Put in a handful of eggshell broken up small, a little ammonia and warm water, shake and leave for some hours; rinse.

4 Put in to a height of about 5 cm (2 in) a 5% solution of nitric or sulphuric acid which you have had made up by a chemist. Swill round for a few minutes, empty and give plentiful rinsing.

   *Warning*: wear rubber gloves and take care to avoid splashes to eyes or exposed skin. See general safety note on page 6.

5 Put in a handful of small lead shot, or coarse sand, and swill it about; this should loosen awkward deposits.

In some districts water jugs become cloudy when they take on a fine deposit of lime. Removal is simple: fill with distilled water or rain water and leave to stand for about a week. The cloudiness should then come away by wiping with a coarse rag or a little gentle brushing.

## Washing glass

This should be carried out one piece at a time, as with ceramics, in a plastic bowl filled with water comfortably hot to the hands, plus a little good quality detergent, having placed a piece of plastic foam at the bottom of the bowl. A few drops of ammonia may be added to the washing water. Rinse in luke-warm water and dry as recommended under *Drying*.

# Metals

In no other division of antiques are there such intricate problems for anyone bent on their care. There are alloys, pure metals, particular hazards to contend with and, to complicate it more, craftsmen for over fourty centuries have used a large number of often strange and wonderful techniques on their creations.

Where to start? The basic metals. At the head of the line the noblest of them all. Gold, that precious, almost magic stuff, that will not tarnish. If an object which claims to be gold is exhibiting a tarnish – it isn't pure. Something else has been slipped into it. Gold will not corrode. Although it may be found with incrustations of lime, these will come away with a few touches of a cotton bud dipped in a 1% solution of nitric acid and attachments of clay can be washed off with lukewarm water with a little gentle detergent. Gold objects may also be come across with a form of red patina which may have resulted from heating at one time in their life. There are also golds that have been intentionally coloured by the addition of additives; tints include: blue, green and red. This is something precious, particularly with coins, and if removed it is nearly impossible to re-create. Apart from objects of solid pure gold, the beautiful metal has been employed to decorate armour, weapons, silver dishes, caskets, illuminated manuscripts, jewellery and countless other rare pieces. There it is the king metal. The others most frequently found, either by themselves or in alloys, include aluminium, antimony, bismuth, chromium, copper, iron, lead, nickel, platinum, silver, tin and zinc.

## An ABC of alloys

The alloys that are bred from these metals include:

### Ashbury metal
A hard pewter, containing antimony, tin and zinc. Used for snuff-boxes and cheap spoons and forks.

### Babbitt's metal
A bronze with a high tin content, plus the copper and some antimony. Invented by Isaac Babbitt (1799–1862).

### Bidri
Another pewter, also the family name for the pieces made from it largely at Bidar near Hyderabad in India. The composition included tin, zinc, and a little each of copper and lead. The surface of the objects was engraved and silver and gold were inlaid into the lines, the surface being wiped with ammonia and saltpetre to blacken the pewter.

### Brass
At first an alloy of copper and generally tin, but modern brass would approximate to two parts copper and one part zinc; sometimes traces of other metals might be added to give particular characteristics.

### Britannia metal
At the outset produced about 1770 by James Vickers of Sheffield and made from copper, antimony and tin. Early pieces looked like pewter. Plating on Britannia metal was introduced in the 1820s; the intention was probably that it should be taken for Sheffield plate.

### Bronze
One of the oldest of all alloys; the Bronze Age began in the Middle East about 4,500BC. Constituents have included: copper, tin, zinc, lead and phosphorus. Bronze is used widely with sculpture and many techniques with antiques.

### Cast iron
High carbon iron that is too brittle to forge. Objects produced from it are moulded whilst molten. There was a vogue for chairs and tables to be made with it in America around the mid-19th century.

### Cock metal
A soft alloy, which could be made from copper and lead or other

base metals. A slang term implying a low-grade alloy, one most likely to be used for cheap items or shoddy reproductions.

### Electrum
A natural or man-made alloy of gold and silver, much used for jewellery and decorative work.

### German silver
A 19th-century introduction to imitate silver with jewellery and tableware. Made from copper, zinc and nickel. Other names include: nickel silver and white silver, and also paktong which is a Chinese variation.

### Latten
Not really a true alloy. A metal sheet hammered out from brass or a close-to-brass alloy. A favourite material with early locksmiths.

### Ley
A poor quality pewter with a very high lead content. At one time it must have been responsible for a drop in population as wine measures were apparently made from it, and the acid from the beverage would produce a dangerous blend.

### Pewter
An alloy with tin as the principal component, although early pewters had a preponderance of lead. Romans were producing it certainly in the 3rd century and probably quite a bit before that. The earliest Roman pewter found in Britain was a tin and lead lethal variety. A thousand or more years later the meats for Edward I's coronation were boiled in great pewter cauldrons. More modern pewters have dropped the lead and substituted copper and antimony. (See also Ashbury metal, Bidri.)

### Pinchbeck
First made from copper and zinc by Christopher Pinchbeck around 1700. Intended to ape gold for cheap jewellery, it has been used by poor class fakers.

### Prince's metal
Said to have been invented by Prince Rupert, Count Palatine of the Rhine (1619–82). Largely made of copper with a little zinc, the idea was that it would fool people that it was gold.

*Spelter*
Low-grade pewter type alloy; zinc and a small proportion of lead.
Also specialised solder of zinc and copper.

*Steel*
Alloys of iron with carbon, and also possibly traces of phosphorus, manganese, chromium, sulphur and nickel.

*Tula*
Made at Tula in Russia from silver, copper and lead for filling the incisions in niello work.

*White iron*
A hard silvery-white cast iron. Sheet iron coated with tin.

*Wrought iron*
This has a very low carbon content and is tough and malleable; often used for decorative work.

## General care of metals and alloys

The main point to remember with metals and alloys is that it can be easy to go too far and cause damage that will be difficult if not impossible to reverse. There are quite a number of recipes around which, quite honestly, are more concerned with a pretty flashy end result and which have little concern for the welfare of the object being treated. There are the polish-at-all-costs characters who seize on some old pewter with a patina that has taken 400 years to grow. They reach for metal polish 'A' that may have a strong abrasive action, and smothering the pewter with this, buff it up by hand or worse still, use an electric polisher. They only stop when the unfortunate piece is gleaming and sparkling in a passable imitation of silver. Another such fellow would take an early medieval sword that was pitted with rust and subject it to a grinding with an emery wheel, until the blade, somewhat slimmer, reappeared glimmering as almost-new steel.

The care of metal has nothing in common with these approaches. It is to try to conserve what is there, and to give treatments that will complement the characteristics of the metals and alloys that have been used with varying techniques. The methods included below are reasonably safe if carefully followed. But whenever possible make tests on small areas underneath or out-of-sight. Have a neutralizing agent ready to hand.

# Materials, problems, products and processes

## Abrasives

Risky materials in this field. To prove the point, take a piece of scrap metal and give it a rub with an abrasive powder, wash it off and look what has happened. There will be an obvious mark where the powder was applied. Now try and get rid of it.

There are a number of very fine abrasive powders such as: crocus, Tripoli (see WHERE TO GET WHAT), pumice, putty, whiting and jeweller's rouge (see page 80). These can be helpful for removing rust spots from armour that is otherwise in good order or small stains from corrosion or incrustation on metals and alloys. For a perfect job, the areas should be given a controlled burnishing afterwards with a bloodstone or similar hard polishing stone, obtainable from an art shop or jewellers' supplies.

There are special cloths available that have been impregnated with certain abrasive materials; these are obtainable from good ironmongers.

## Adhesives

The introduction of epoxy resin adhesives tailored to particular materials has made for great advances in dealing with endangered metal. Select the right one and breakages can be made good which would have been impossible before. Principal points to watch for are that rust and tarnish should be removed first and the areas to be joined should be thoroughly degreased with methylated spirits. Consolidation can be effected from the back or in a place that will not show, by using a quite large dab of an epoxy, either by itself to strengthen, or as a footing for a brace. Casting-resins with metallic fillers have proved successful for the building up of badly corroded areas. Their grey-black tone corresponds well with ferrous metals and can be given a most convincing metallic lustre by rubbing up with steel wool.

## Alloys, lesser

The pinchbecks, the Britannias and the rest can be treated broadly in the manner employed for the alloy or metal which they seem set on imitating. The finished effect, with many of these, may be variable, as their constituents often differ. But they should all come up with a good polish and take a lacquer or wax coating.

## Aluminium

Really a newcomer to the antique field, but as the cut-out date for antiques creeps forward, assisted by the needs of the auction rooms, objects are coming up that have been worked this century in this rather odd metal. It can be strangely unsympathetic to cleaning and polishing. With an object that was stained and where there were no other metals or other materials present, one lady I heard of got excellent results by brewing up rhubarb leaves and the tops of the stalks with water. Then she dipped a swab of cotton wool in this and laid it on the offending areas, and after a short period and perhaps a wave of some hidden wand, when the swab was lifted off there was no stain.

*Warning*: Green rhubarb and in particular its leaves do contain quite a supply of oxalic acid, which is highly poisonous.

To polish aluminium, one of those soft impregnated cloths will give as good a result as any.

## Ammonia

Although it is often referred to as an all-purpose cleaner, with some metals and alloys, particularly bronze, it can cause much trouble. At dilute strengths it can, however, assist when mixed with other cleaning materials.

## Anti-tarnish papers

These are useful when storing silver, particularly in urban and industrial areas, and they will give considerable protection. The silver should be given a cleaning just before wrapping up and must be absolutely dry. There are also anti-tarnish cloths intended for the same purpose.

## Arms and armour

These can be complicated to clean because, certainly with firearms, several materials can be present: different metals and alloys, woods and inlays of bone, ivory and mother-of-pearl. If it is possible, the ideal way to cope with this problem is to dis-assemble the pieces and then to deal with each as suggested under the headings given here or in other chapters. But this is not always advisable due to age, fragility and corrosion, so con-sider this course carefully beforehand. Once a decision to go ahead has been taken, the way to do so is by using cotton buds and a quality masking tape.

## Brass

Old brass should, where possible, have the patina preserved and not ground away with coarse hard abrasive powders or polishes. Obstinate marks can be tackled with jeweller's rouge (see page 80) mixed to a liquid paste with a little paraffin; another recipe which can be more gentle still is fine white wood ash, carefully sifted for any lumps, mixed with methylated spirits. Severe corrosion may be shifted with a strong washing soda solution, and this may even be taken as far as boiling the objects in the solution.

*Warning*: Wear rubber gloves to protect eyes and skin.

Oxalic acid will also do the job. Get your chemist to mix up for you 15 g (½oz) of oxalic acid with 1 l (1¾ pints) of warm water. Either dip the piece in this solution for about three minutes, or sluice the acid solution over it with an old dish-mop, then in either case rinse very thoroughly.

*Warning*: Remember oxalic acid is highly poisonous. For obstinate tarnish a few drops of weak ammonia mixed with the jeweller's rouge or wood ash can help. Rinse well.

To protect brass once polished and particularly if it is an outside door knocker or other such piece there are a number of commercial lacquers (see PRODUCTS). These, depending on brand, can give fair protection for up to three months. They should then be removed with either acetone or methylated spirits, as advised on the bottle, and reapplied. When putting on lacquer, hold the piece up and against the light so that it can be seen if any areas are missed. Brass may also be protected by applying a very thin coat of fine white wax polish (see PRODUCTS).

## Bronze

Here the approach should be very cautious for often this attractive alloy has been used to make the rare and valuable; indeed it has been in use for around four thousand years for many purposes and for longer still for weapons and domestic items. Again, it is that elusive veiling, the patina, that must be cared for. Scour that away and watch the noughts drop off the value figure. It needs an experienced eye to look at a dark piece of bronze and to be able to tell whether the tone is the grime of history or whether it was intentionally put there by the craftsman. Dust first with a soft brush and then examine again. If there are accretions of greasy dirt in the details, try to ease these out with a brush dipped in white spirit. There are objects of bronze that were polished originally and these may be treated in the same way as brass, always selecting a polish that is gentle and not just a scourer. Protection by lacquering or waxing is mainly one of aesthetics, and it can always be removed if disliked.

### Bronze disease

This can be an outbreak of rather rough tiny light-green spots, which can also attack brass. The onslaught is generally caused by the presence of chlorides which react with dampness and the presence of oxygen and so cause corrosion and deterioration of the alloys. Some bronzes have a green-blue patina applied to them so don't be confused. The 'disease' is quite definitely an outbreak of pimples and not an overall veiling. If the piece is of value the cure here should be in the hands of an expert.

## Cast iron
See *Iron*

## Champlevé

An enamelling process in which small depressions or cells are first cut into the supporting metal, generally copper, and then into these are put enamel pastes and the whole is then fired. Examine with a magnifying glass and see if the enamels are secure. If they are secure, it is possible to wash them gently with a good quality soap and lukewarm water, gently easing into the design with a soft paint brush. If there is grease present the brush can be dipped into white spirit.

It has been found that though many enamels are strong and not affected by knocks, some may be under internal strain and can become loosened. If this is noticed it should be treated at once, as the fracturing and loosening can spread. Prepare some dilute lacquer (see PRODUCTS) and flood on so that it goes well in and round all the small enamelled pieces. Another attempt at consolidation can be to use a dilute synthetic water-clear glue in the same way.

## Chasing

The decoration of a metal surface by the use of a small special chasing hammer and punches and chisels. If the delicate marks become unacceptably filled with grime, use a soft brush and white spirit to clean out.

## Chromium

Another metal that is primarily associated with 20th-century objects. It will almost certainly mainly be met with as a plating, often on copper, sometimes on iron or steel. Rust stains can be removed with proprietary cleaners and there are several adequate polishes to be had (see PRODUCTS). Remember that you are dealing with a plating which can be very thin indeed so don't use abrasives, as they will go through, and that rather pleasant looking sheen of a red-yellow metal will be the copper underneath. If just dirty, wash with a soft cloth and soapy water; if there are discolorations, add a little ammonia to the washing water. Rinse in clear water and dry well.

## Cloisonné

An enamelling method that goes back to the Byzantine period of the 6th century and may be of far older origin. With this, tiny fences of metal, sometimes gold or silver, were soldered to the support metal. Then into these small fenced areas the enamel pastes were placed and then fired. The effect of the slender hairs of gold or silver between the translucent enamel colours can be of great richness. Treat as for *Champlevé*.

## Coins

In general the cleaning of these should be left to a trained hand, as it is easy to cause damage that cannot be rectified. Mention has been made of a heat patina with gold. Similar veilings of time are often looked on with respect by collectors and should not be disturbed unless the whole matter is well understood. The removal of corrosion is a sensitive problem which is best solved in a laboratory. The use of acids and strong alkalis are out.

## Copper

To the treatments mentioned for brass there are some other ways that can be suggested. Using a proprietary electro-chemical dip (see PRODUCTS) is safe with one important proviso. Never dip a copper piece into a container of dip that has been used for silver or another metal, or else there will be trouble with possibly a form of cross-plating. Verdigris will generally submit to an application of a solution of 15 g (½ oz) of citric acid in 600 ml (1 pint) of warm water. Stir this until completely dissolved, then either dip the piece, or sponge the liquid over it, and follow this by rinsing first with weak warm soapy water and then just warm water, and lastly dry thoroughly. Small patches of verdigris can be treated with a paste of white vinegar and salt; rinse thoroughly afterwards.

Pure copper has the most attractive warm, almost crimson-brick-red blush on the surface. Try to effect the polishing so that it is purely a surface treatment and not a harsh rubbing that will obscure this special copper look.

## Corrosion

Basically this is the loss of metallic qualities and the appearance of incrustations that can be caused by a variety of chemical reactions. Many metallic objects buried in the soil emerge with some evidence of corrosion. In the house probably the commonest example can be found by looking inside a silver salt cellar, if it has no proper glass liner, and also at a silver salt spoon if left for long uncleaned. It does not take much spillage of salt combined with damp to eat through even the finest example of the work of that eminent 18th-century woman silversmith, Hester Bateman. If an outbreak is observed on any metal, brush or wash off what you can and then thoroughly dry. Keep dry, and as soon as possible ask for professional help. Old recipes for removal can often do more harm that provide a cure.

## Damascening

A sensitive method for decorating metals by inlaying other, often precious, metals and hammering the surface to lock them into place. A dulled surface can generally be brought up by an application of 2% nitric acid (made up by your chemist) mixed with methylated spirits, in the proportions of 30 ml (1 fl oz) nitric acid to 142 ml (5 fl oz) methylated spirits. Wearing rubber gloves, soak a large swab of cotton wool in this liquid and sluice quickly over the surface to be treated, leaving the acid solution on no longer than a few seconds; immediately give a thorough rinse in ample quantities of water. After the damascene has been well dried the surface can be given a sparse coating of a quality white wax polish (see PRODUCTS) or a little lanolin dressing. Give a light buffing and then feel it to be sure that all evidence of tackiness has gone, as if this is left it will attract dirt from the atmosphere.

## Dents

A questionable area for do-it-yourself. Removal of even slight knocks can be a tricky one and the best silver teapot should be treated by a craftsman. There are so many specialist tools involved and such knowledge of metalwork it is better not to attempt it as an unskilled blow with a hammer can make the situation worse.

### Engine turning

A form of often mechanical patterning, or decorative process as made by a rose engine, that can be applied to a flat surface such as a visiting-card holder or a cigarette case to assist gripping the object and also to protect it from abrasion when being carried in the pocket or handbag. If it is a little deep and accretions of dirt accumulate it can be cleaned with a medium hard brush and a polishing paste.

### Engraving

Decoration worked by a craftsman, usually with a hard pointed graver gouging out tiny slivers of metal. Found on many metal objects, particularly armour. The graver lines can be cleaned out with a polish worked in with a brush. Be careful afterwards to see that all polish is removed, as small remains can be unsightly and if left will harden in.

### Etching

Another quite common method of decorating metals; it will be found on armour, and also door plates and silver. The method is that the craftsman first covers the area to be decorated with a protective ground of a resin and a wax. Then he needles through his design and applies an acid, which is generally nitric or a corrosive mordant. The line produced varies from the engraved line, which is more or less a 'V'-shaped furrow. The etched line will be 'U'- shaped and may, if the acid has been left on too long, have 'crevassed' or undercut each side. Because of this, etched work should be examined carefully and handled with care, for with old pieces the edges of the lines can be fragile. Cleaning out can be as for engraving.

### German silver

Treat with silver polish (see PRODUCTS) but not one of the 'dip' type.

### Gilding on metals

Dealing with ormolu has been discussed under FURNITURE. If found used in other ways on metals, it should be treated with great respect, as the actual layer of gold is less than wafer thin. The methods for ormolu should be safe.

# Iron

This metal, cast, wrought or as the alloy steel, can give some trouble. Damp is the number one foe, for after not very long exposure the most pristine surfaces can start to show a blush of red-brown, the first onset of iron oxide, rust. If caught in the early stages it will easily be removed by a wash over with paraffin or a proprietary rust remover; rinse afterwards with white spirit, dry very thoroughly and give some protection to the metal by applying a white wax polish as with *Damascening*.

If the rust is deep-seated, there may well be unsightly pitting. This really amounts to a metallic loss. Remove surface rust and clean up as best you can; never try to abrade out the pitting, as you will wreck what is left of the sword or helmet.

Where iron articles such as cast-iron fenders are in good condition, commercial shot blasting is permissible (see WHERE TO GET WHAT). As soon as possible after this treatment, apply a coat of quality white wax polish, lanolin or a special lacquer. As to which of these protectors is used will depend on the function of the object and the desired appearance. As an added help to the final look, the piece can be slightly warmed prior to the application of the chosen finish.

# Jeweller's rouge

Although mentioned under abrasives, it does warrant a separate word of caution. Be careful when using it not to get any of the powder under the nails or worked into the quicks, as it can cause rather nasty inflammation. Wear rubber gloves or rub a barrier cream into fingers and round nails.

# Lacquer

There are a number of commercial lacquers (see PRODUCTS). Some may state they can be used on any metal, but it is better to get one that specifies a particular metal. Lacquers can be applied by brush or spray.

*Warning*: as most of them have a fairly strong smell that may be toxic for certain people, apply where there is good ventilation.

# Lead

Most likely to be found cast as garden statuettes, sometimes also as applied ornaments to wooden balusters on a stairway. Apart from a going-over with a fairly stiff bristle brush to remove dust and grime, it is best left alone. The blue-grey-green patina is attractive but very frail and any abrasive cleaning or liquid polishing would wreck it. If showing signs of odd growths, it should if possible be brought inside to an area which is warm and then left to dry well out before being given the brush treatment. For some, a light waxing over with quality white polish is acceptable and this can be a protective measure; if not liked it can be wiped off with swabs of cotton wool dipped into white spirit.

*Warning*: after working with lead, wash hands very thoroughly.

## Niello
The skilled art of filling chased or engraved work with a black composition. This should be treated with respect. It is not unknown for some enthusiastic cleaner to work away with wire brushes, steel wool, hard bristle scrubbing brushes and a fearsome array of liquid cleaners in a desperate attempt to get that nasty black mess out of those pretty lines. Result, bang goes another piece of fine craftsmanship.

Pliny the Elder mentions that the technique was employed in Egypt and there are daggers from Mycenae well over three thousand years old bearing this kind of decoration. The point is that any cleaning of anything bearing niello has to be done with considerable care. Surface polishing is safer than dipping, and the cloths should be soft and brushes should not be used.

## Ormolu
See under FURNITURE

## Patina
This subtle feature has a different nature from a patina on wood or other substances. It is less definable and, if anything, more gentle. Often, as with bronze, the artist may have created an artificial patina by chemical washing or other treatment.

## Pewter
One of those difficult ones. Certainly it should never be given a massive polish. Some even advocate that all it needs is a dusting and a gentle rubbing up with a soft chamois. A mild further treatment can be to take a rag and dip it into a light clear oil and rumple it around in the hands until it is evenly dispersed; then dip it into some crocus powder (see GLOSSARY) or other very fine powder and work this gently over the piece. Wipe off the oil with some cotton wool dipped in methylated spirits and lastly wash, rinse and dry.

Old pewter may sometimes have small spots somewhat similar

to the look of bronze disease. It is likely that the cause is from a contamination with salts; and also there may be signs of corrosion. If the piece is valuable, take it along to a trained man. Otherwise a remedial treatment can be tried.

*Removing spots*
Make up a dilute solution of sodium hydroxide (caustic soda) in the proportions of 30 g (1 oz) to 4.5l (1 gall) in a plastic bowl to a depth sufficient to submerge the object.

*Warning*: wear rubber gloves, a resistant apron and goggles for this one and check first with warning note on page 6.

Lower the piece in so that it is covered and if hollow is filled with the solution. Leave for a few minutes, lift out with laundry tongs and inspect and put back again until satisfied. Remove and very thoroughly rinse in several waters. Dry and use the chamois to gently sheen the surface. Detailed pewter that is heavily grimed may be treated with a soft brush and quality soap suds.

The susceptibility of pewter to 'rough' liquids is often put to good use by the back-room workers. I have seen two of them studiously concocting the look of the 17th century for today's pewter. A bath of goodness knows what; jugs, mugs and measures being lowered into same tied in bundles by their handles. Fumes arising, bubbling and hissing. Brought out, looked at, and lowered again until the 'right date' was reached; then a bit of a knocking about, perhaps even the addition of a 'touch' mark, although they seldom bother as most of the customers wouldn't know what it was anyway.

**Planishing**
The smoothing or surfacing of a metal by light hammering. This may leave a subtle unevenness. Polish with soft cloths to avoid bringing up the tiny dimples with a too-high shine which would spoil the effect of this finish.

**Platinum**
Nearly as untarnishable as gold, platinum is mainly liable to be affected by chlorine and sulphur. To clear, make a gentle application of jeweller's rouge (see page 80) with either a few drops of light oil or methylated spirits. Often simulated by alloys of white gold, in which can be palladium, gold, silver, nickel or copper; and also attempts may be made to pass off steel with traces of nickel and possibly silver.

## Pointillé
Decoration that is made by pricking or the use of finely pointed punches. Cleaning may be done with standard polishes and the use of a medium brush, finishing with a chamois.

## Polishing
The intention should be to bring up the full quality of the metal or alloy. To do this, it is not necessary to use vast quantities of liquids or pastes. Apply in general lightly, using a brush if the decoration demands it, and buff up with clean soft cloths or a good chamois. Always look at the cleaning cloths first to be sure that they have not picked up any gritty particles. For soft delicate metals wear cotton gloves, as it is surprising how a tiny piece of hard skin can mar a surface. If in doubt about an untried polish, take a little and rub between a thumb and forefinger to feel the harshness or softness of whatever abrasive material it may have in it. If not quite certain, compare with known safe preparations such as jeweller's rouge or crocus powder (see WHERE TO GET WHAT).

Burnishers like bloodstone or agates should only be used with reservation, perhaps on a lesser piece to ease out a small blemish. These are obtainable from art shops or jewellers' suppliers.

## Prince's metal
If recognised, treat as for brass.

## Repoussé
A method for decorating some metals, notably silver, pewter and tin, and also sometimes gold, by hammering from the back to produce a design in relief. When cleaning and polishing, treat rather in the manner of planishing (see opposite) so that undue prominence is not given to the hammer's marks. A large very soft brush can be a help. Another device which will serve and also be of use with other metals is a 'rubber'. To make one, cut a chamois into strips about 8 cm (3 in) wide. Roll these lengthwise into a fat cylinder of around 5 cm (2 in) in diameter and bind in the middle with string (*see diagram on following page*). Time taken in making two of these 'rubbers' will be well spent. One can be used to put on a polish and the other for polishing. They will certainly help considerably to bring up a special and attractive finish on the surface skin of repoussé, and also on chased and engraved pieces.

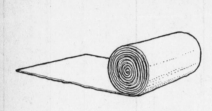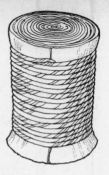

*Diagram 9  Making a 'rubber' to polish repoussé and other metals*

## Scratches, treating

The 'rubbers' mentioned above are suitable tools to use with one of the super-fine powders such as crocus or Tripoli (see WHERE TO GET WHAT) or jeweller's rouge (see page 80) to tackle shallow unsightly scratching. Mix the chosen powder with a few drops of light oil, dip the 'rubber' into this and apply with gentle but firm circular strokes. Another trick can be to use a large stick of velvet-soft charcoal, similar to that which an artist uses when removing a blemish from an etching plate. This should be about 2–3 cm (1 in) across and if possible of vine charcoal (from art shops).

## Sheffield plate

The orginal technique was evolved in 1742 by Thomas Bolsover. Basically this was the rolling of a thin sheet of silver under pressure and heat on to a sheet of copper with the addition of a flux. Today the idea is carried out by electrolysis, silver being deposited on the copper. As to which is actually the safest method for cleaning Sheffield plate, there is some argument. Liquid polishes which contain abrasive materials, pastes and powders, are all going to rub away some metal, even if that amount is infinitesimally small. The older Sheffield plates may have a thicker layer or skin of silver. But they too will suffer, for perhaps in their lives more than one heavy hand has ground an emery powder into them to get a quick polish. Present-day fine proprietary polishes, however, are as reliable as these things can be. Put on the liquids or pastes with a soft rag or brush and polish up with more soft cloths or a soft chamois. Wearing cotton gloves will again help to protect the surfaces and indeed your hands. Sheffield plate may also be given an electro-chemical dip (see PRODUCTS). If the copper body is showing through, leave in the liquid for a very short time. Wash afterwards, whether polished or dipped, rinse and dry thoroughly.

## Silver

To many the loveliest metal of all, with an incomparable sheen and subtle quality. It has been known and appreciated for thousands of years, certainly as far back as the Early Sumerian period, around 3500 BC. Silver was a rarity with the early Egyptians; this being pointed to by the fact that the tomb robbers who broke into Tutankhamen's resting place made a grab first for the silver before the gold.

This metal, sadly, is most prone to tarnish as is also, of course, Sheffield plate or silver-plated ware. A dark-brown surface film starts to form, the composition of which is silver sulphide. Among the causes are industrial releases of sulphur dioxide and open fire flues. Other unsuspected sources are such as storage cupboards painted inside with emulsion paints containing casein, as this can have a bacterial action that will release sulphur compounds. Vulcanised rubber draught seals and floor coverings can be guilty too. More unexpected still are clothes and fabrics about the house that have been given certain 'finish' treatments which have a sulphur content; warmth from central heating or the body can set these darkening agents loose.

When handling silver, particularly fine pieces from the 18th century and earlier times, reach for the cotton gloves; apart from damages hinted at under the heading of polishing, they will also protect silver from sweaty fingerprints which at times almost seem to etch themselves into the metal. Clean as for *Sheffield plate*, either with polishes or a 'dip'.

### De-tarnishing treatment

If extreme tarnish is met with, try a reliable but rather alarming looking process.

*Warning*: wear rubber gloves and read warning note on page 6. Have ready a pair of wooden laundry tongs.

Put a piece of aluminium sheet about 20 cm (8 in) square, or about a metre (roughly a yard) of crumpled aluminium cooking foil at the bottom of a large plastic washing up bowl. Now put in the pieces of silver to be cleaned and add enough really hot solution of washing soda – 142 g (5 oz) soda to 600 ml (1 pint) water – to submerge them completely. Don't be alarmed by seeming eruptions issuing from the cauldron. After about a minute, lift out the objects for inspection, using the laundry tongs – don't dip your hands in the solution as you can't depend on the rubber gloves to protect them completely. Detarnishing does not take very long but you may need to repeat the process once or twice. Wash and rinse thoroughly, then dry.

*Storing*

As mentioned earlier, there are both anti-tarnish impregnated papers and cloths, which are useful for storage purposes. Wrap the silver first in tissue paper when using either of these. Silver that is not intended for eating with, or off, can be given a light waxing with a pure white polish; it may be lacquered (see PRODUCTS) or given a patented shield treatment by a firm specialising in this process.

## Stain removal

Stains that do not come away with normal polishing or 'dipping' may be treated by gentle rubbing with fine powders, as recommended under individual entries; use the home-made 'rubber' (see *Repoussé*) with a drop or two of fine oil or use a block of soft charcoal. A pad of cotton wool soaked in 5% oxalic acid left on for a few minutes can help.

*Warning*: get this made up for you and remember, oxalic acid is highly poisonous.

*Fire stain*

Commonly found on brass-handled fire irons and copper kettles and pans. Unless well-seated from age, any good proprietary polish will take it off. If this fails, try the 2% nitric acid and methylated spirits preparation, suggested under *Damascening*, and if necessary follow up with a paste of jeweller's rouge (see page 80) or one of the other mild abrasive powders.

*Silver*

Table silver has three main enemies on our menu: eggs, salt and vinegar. Don't leave silver in contact with foodstuffs for any longer than is necessary. Many ingredients we like other than those just mentioned will also stain or tarnish this metal, so into the washing water speedily. Salt cellars should wherever possible have glass or some kind of liner, but even then wash the silver part after use as it does not take many of those small white particles to set up corrosion.

Silver coffee and teapots do get stained inside, but never follow the ideas of one good country lady who was always in a hurry; she found to her delight that a pad of steel wool would bring it all up nice and clean in seconds. Please use 5 ml (1 tsp) of borax in 600 ml (1 pint) of hot water. Leave this in for up to two hours, then swill round with a soft brush, not forgetting the spout. Empty, wash in warm soapy water, rinse and dry.

## Tin
This may be cleaned with polishes or 'dipped' or be sponged over with 5% oxalic acid (*warning*: highly poisonous). Wash, rinse and dry. A protective coat of fine white wax polish may be given. Some native tin articles may be not quite pure, and in this case leave the surface rather as pewter.

## Verdigris
A hot strong solution of washing soda should remove this from brass; follow the directions given under *Silver, De-tarnishing treatment*, taking the same safety measures. For copper, treat with 15 g (½oz) of citric acid to 600 ml (1 pint) of warm water.

## Wrought iron
Treat as for *Iron*.

# Textiles

The group of materials that come under this heading are nearly as complicated in all their ways as metals. The fibres used include cotton, flax, fur, silk and wool. In some instances other off-beat plant fibres may have been tried. I suppose too that such is the rate of advance in the cut-out date for antiques that man-made fibres will soon be on the list. The various fibres have been spun, woven, knitted, crocheted, dyed, block printed, embroidered and matted, and there have been many little off-shoot individual methods from any one of these or other techniques by experimenting craftworkers.

These oft-times delicate things have had to stand a fairly thorough working-over during their life, what with manhandling, natural hazards and pests, added to the individual weakness of the different types of material. Much harm has often been done to them by lack of know-how. Materials have sometimes been haplessly grouped together for mass treatment, to whirl their way round and round in washing machines. Silks, wools, cottons, linens, felts, laces, embroideries and piled fabrics should always be treated individually. Within these groups are again sub-divisions that call for their own special treatment. Embroidery embraces widely varying types such as broderie anglaise, crewel work, Opus Anglicanum (the English church embroidery that became renowned throughout Europe in the 13th and 14th centuries), petit point, samplers and stumpwork, each of these bringing in many different materials and surface textures, even gold and other metallic threads. Lace may have 50 or more varieties. Silk can appear as the most fragile wisps or as heavy rich cloths. Cotton, linen and wool range from fine materials like muslin to strong heavy fabrics.

Any textiles of whatever age or however they have been used, in hangings, upholstery, applied decoration or costumes, should have thorough and periodic inspection. Yes, and if in doubt, take a good strong magnifying glass to the task. If damage, staining or deterioration is seen, have a notebook handy and put down what wants doing to what. Then on a good dry day, make a determined attempt to deal with those things that are threatening these often lovely materials from the past, often highly personalised: a sampler stitched by a distant relative in 1835; an embroidered waistcoat from the mid-18th century with what appears to be a patch of blood that could have been from the point of a sword, or some really old fragment of woven wool that surprises one that such subtlety of design and tint could have been accomplished then and could have survived at all.

## Materials, problems and processes

*Handling and display*
As a general rule handle textiles with great respect and give those of advanced years all the care you can. The outward appearance can be misleading because the deterioration of tensile strength in the threads may not be evident on a casual examination. After often centuries of exposure to changing atmospheric conditions these still lovely old fabrics can have lost much of their original resilience. Items such as tapestries or rugs which are to be hung on a wall should be done so from a roller or bar. The attachment should be by sewn tapes or by using loops or other devices that are already on the piece. Never start driving iron tacks or the like through the materials. Large carpets, rugs or tapestries should be rolled, preferably round a large cardboard cylinder when they are to be moved or stored; they should never be folded.

Banners or flags that have been weakened by exposure to the elements may be supported by backing with a fine nylon net; if this is sewn on carefully it will still allow the flag to drape and hang correctly from an indoor display mast and the supporting net will be invisible from about three yards off. This nylon net may also be used to strengthen lace, fragile embroideries at the back and other fabrics too weak to be displayed alone. If items are framed they may be either stitched to the nylon net or directly on to a backing material that may be anything favoured for effect. (See also under *Costumes* for displaying these.)

### Ancient textiles
Just where the date should be set is very much an arguable point. But probably those fabrics prior to around 1500 could be classed as such, for except for odd cases, by now they will most likely

have become weak in the fibres and fragile in almost every aspect. As a middle group for age the period between 1500 and 1700 could be chosen, but here also will be found a high degree of fragility, although there will be many more examples remaining in a reasonably good condition. For the first and second groups, any attention should always be given by an expert. Handling should be done with the greatest care. Don't dream of using any preparations that promise instant and wonderful results. These tired old fibres will be brittle and weakened and must be left to the relaxing and conserving methods waiting for them in a laboratory.

## Carpets and rugs

These may be knotted or woven and fibres can range from goat's hair to wool or silk. The basis will be warps and wefts which pass alternately under and over each other. The pile may be coarse or of considerable fineness. But however they are made they have one thing in common: of almost all antique objects they have taken, and are still taking, the most consistently punishing treatment. Think of all those feet that have trodden across them: the mailed step of the knights, the scuff of wooden soles, harsh nailed heels, dogs' and cats' claws, down to stiletto heels. They often take the brunt of spillage and as well have the legs of heavy pieces of furniture crushed into them. Most dust and dirt that flows in through windows and doors eventually beds down into the carpets and rugs. Much of this dirt can well be gritty and the particles sharp to the extent that if it is trampled in for too long, fibres can be seriously weakened and broken. The dirt should be regularly removed, not only for a carpet's or rug's sake but also for yours. If the piece is delicate, it should be gently brushed with a good fine bristle brush and the muck collected with a dustpan. But most carpets and rugs can be cleaned with a carpet sweeper or, for a more thorough job, a vacuum cleaner. Whichever way, however, is used, avoid any undue pulling at the tufts or heavy pressure down into the carpet with the head of the cleaner. This idea that the more pressure exerted the better and more thorough the cleaning will be, is really a bit of a myth. For if the fan-shaped head of the cleaner is pushed really hard down on to the pile it can have the effect of flattening it to such a degree that the dirt it is seeking to extract will be imprisoned.

Do, as far as possible, have some kind of protective cup under legs and castors. The Dutch have a pleasant habit with rugs; they quite often put them on tables. If you are storing away carpets and rugs, see that there is some kind of insect repellant (see *Insect pests*) placed with them and, as previously mentioned, always roll rather than fold.

If the corners do develop a curl, which is not only unsightly but also a risk for an unwary foot, this is best treated by an application of starch from the back. Such a course is better than other ideas that include: latex, sticking on pieces of lino and even, sacrilege, tacking down to the boards.

## Testing for colour fastness

Before any treatment other than brushing and vacuuming is undertaken the carpet or rug should be carefully examined for colour fastness. This should be done preferably at an edge and at the back. To make a test, dab a little soap and water solution on to the carpet or rug to be washed, leave it for about two minutes and then press a piece of clean white blotting paper into the damp spot; if the blotting paper comes away clear it should be safe to continue. Once assured that all is fast, most can be given a gentle and mild shampooing, using either one of the proprietary carpet shampoos or water and a little good quality fine solid or liquid soap. Don't try and work over the whole carpet at once; move across taking on not more than $\frac{1}{4}$sq m (2–3sq ft) at a time. Don't over wet, and have plenty of cloths wrung out both for the soaping and the rinsing. Have also separate buckets for the soapy water and the rinsing water. It is better to do this task on a fine day, and a draught from a reversed vacuum cleaner will help in the drying. As far as possible move the furniture out of the way.

## Washing a precious rug

If fastness is confirmed, it is possible also to thoroughly wash rugs. You need a plastic or enamelled bath into which the rug can be lowered with a series of folds but without any crumpling, or undue squeezing up. The water need only be lukewarm and whatever soap is chosen it should be completely dissolved and dispersed before putting the rug in. If it is at all delicate, lower the rug into the water supported by a piece of string netting, not old fishing net, as it may still have some dressing in it that could transfer to your prize Persian rug. Gently knead all over with fingers or with a well-rounded piece of wood at least 12 cm (5 in) in diameter. Lift the rug out on the net; let out the dirty water, refill the bath with clean water and lower in the rug; again gently knead. Repeat the rinsing at least three times as it is essential to get rid of all the soap.

After lifting out the last time, spread out the rug in its natural shape on the netting and hang up to dry as near flat as possible. If you can, rig up some aerial defence from passing birds because when they have been feasting on certain fruits their evacuations can be potent. I know one instance of a lady who had done everything quite right. She had even given five rinses. She then set up the pleasant little peasant rug to dry on its net. Over flies a blackbird slightly inebriated with the lady's fruits and a few minutes later she was bewailing the appearance of a large bleached mark on part of the red ground. Not an easy condition to remedy other than by tiresome touching in with a dye which will need to match and this can be very difficult. See also *Stain removal.*

Should carpets require more treatment than already indicated, this is best left to a professional, as are also both rugs and carpets if the dyes are not fast.

## Costumes

Hidden in battered cardboard boxes and corded family trunks stacked away up in the attic are sometimes treasured reminders of how our great-great-greats looked when dressed. The sheer quality of some of the materials and the exquisite workmanship are a wonder beside most similar garments today. Often these old objects will have been wrapped away tightly packed in tissue paper and with a handful of the old moth balls. Although heavily creased, they may emerge in good condition, spotlessly clean; evidence that somebody cared. Nevertheless they are more than likely to have suffered some stain or other attack over the years. The principal dangers for them come from the presence of dirt when they were put away, the approach of damp, packed in airtight enclosures, and hungry insect grubs; then when they emerge over-strong light will continue the damage.

Wherever possible storage should be in dry and well ventilated places that are not likely to be subjected to sudden variations in temperature. Garments should be placed in individual polythene bags and have the area around the hanger protected with a roll of tissue paper; for certain examples a similar protection should be given to the shoulders and sleeves. If pieces are unsuitable for hanging they should be put away either rolled or with tissue paper pads placed in the folds. If the natural atmosphere tends towards damp, small containers of silica gel can be hung in muslin bags in places where they will be near to, but not touching, any of the garments.

*Protecting against pests and moulds*

If there is any evidence of a colony of clothes moths or other such nuisances trying to establish themselves, they can be efficiently discouraged quite simply. Place a saucer of paradichlorobenzene crystals in the wardrobe or cupboard; if it is possible rig up a fairly low wattage electric bulb underneath, but not touching, the saucer or the clothes (*see diagram 10*). Seal the cupboard or wardrobe and switch on and leave for 48 hours. Switch off and leave for another 24 hours before opening up. Camphor and naphthalene may be put in small muslin bags and hung in the storage place, again near to, but not touching, the clothes.

One other safeguard for long life. A musty damp smell may be noticed that could be a warning for possible mould growths in the offing. Preventive treatment here can be to place thymol crystals in a saucer, again if possible over a lamp in the same way as the antipest method described above. Switch on for about twenty-four hours and then re-open and ventilate. Be sure that the room itself is well ventilated at the same time.

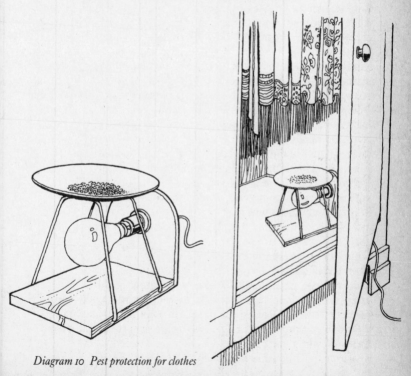

*Diagram 10  Pest protection for clothes*

## Displaying costumes

Old costumes can make attractive display items for certain rooms with unusual features. There may be a large alcove that can be fitted with a glazed door. Wire and padding lay figures can be quite simply made, or an old tailor's dummy used to support a gown or breeches, waistcoat and jacket. Papier mâché face shells and hands can be found, a wig, and you can have an almost natural representation. Even think in terms of taking it a step farther and put beside the figure a small correct period table; have on it perhaps something she or he might have used, drunk or been associated with. Have a light, but not too strong, and some presence of chemicals suggested above aimed at pests. One hotel I know has a fully uniformed dragoon guard in a room, which is so lifelike that people have been know to apologise if they bump into him. (See also *Dry cleaning, Insect pests, Stain removal, Ironing* and *Washing*.)

## Dry cleaning

Rare textiles and those of value should be left to the professional if they need a thorough cleaning. As to commercial High Street cleaners, the approach should be with care. Find out, if you can, exactly what their indemnity position is and what their methods will be. This point is made as it is not unknown for a garment of quality to be taken to a quite select cleaner and a horror to be returned. There was an instance of a beautiful patterned silk stole, probably dating from around 1850 to 1870 that was accepted blandly for cleaning by a well-set-up establishment. When it was returned neatly wrapped up it was unfortunately not examined until in the home. Tragedy – for when opened out it was wrecked; something in the cleaning liquids had reacted with the lovely blues and the areas where these had been had just disappeared, rotted completely away.

If in doubt as to where to entrust a precious item, it is worth asking the advice of a museum that specialises in textiles.

## Dry cleaning at home

If undertaking dry cleaning yourself, always make a test for colour fastness; in general dry cleaning liquids are less likely to affect the materials than water. Lightly dab a little white spirit in an out-of-the-way place on the garment, then hold a piece of clean white blotting paper against this for a short time; if it comes away without a mark it should be safe to proceed.

*Warning*: white spirit is probably the safest effective dry cleaning liquid, but even so, it is highly inflammable. Take fire pre-cautions.

Have a flat tray which will allow for a depth of liquid to 5 cm (2 in) or similar container. Place the garment in this as near flat as possible, or if too big fold over as necessary. Pour white spirit over the piece so that it is covered, then, wearing rubber gloves, gently knead over the whole with fingertips. When satisfied the garment is clean, lift out and hang with some kind of support to thoroughly dry out, on a verandah, open porch or suchlike place.

## Embroidery

There are problems here, not because of the various types to be met with, but because of their various uses: part of a hanging; upholstery on the seat or back of a chair; used as a covering for a trinket box; part of a costume, or an ornamental piece such as a sampler. Apart from silks, wools, cottons and metallic threads, there may be present odd bits of ivory, bone, leather, pieces of shell and metal. If the design is intricate, with a number of these different materials, any cleaning method will have to be used with great care, using small splints of wood with wisps of cotton wool to apply the varying cleaning materials called for. Much can probably be done by a controlled mopping with swabs of cotton wool dipped in white spirit. Often quite heavy grime can be also removed with potato flour, obtainable from a good grocer or chemist. This should be heated to comfortable hand warmth and applied over the face surface of the piece being cleaned. Tamp it down to a 1 cm (½ in) deep layer and leave it on for around ten minutes. Brush off carefully with a soft-hair brush and if neces-sary repeat the treatment.

A dip that is used for silver (see PRODUCTS) can be applied to silver thread, but every care must be taken to see that the dip does not get on to any parts of the fabric. Dilute ammonia can be applied to gold thread in the same way and with the same pre-cautions. Other materials such as bone and shell could also be treated with a weak solution of ammonia, taking due precautions.

Pieces of comparatively thin embroidery such as samplers may, if sound, be washed in a shallow tray with good quality soap flakes and copious rinsing; but don't overlook taking a colour fastness test first. The same object could also be dry cleaned in a tray with white spirit. After any liquid treatment, spread the piece out on a flat surface and gently ease it out to its correct shape and leave to dry. It is permissible to pin out the corners if they turn up, but be certain to use non-rusting pins.

## Insect pests

The principal criminal with textiles and associated materials is the clothes moth, the grub of which will contentedly munch its way through wool, soft cotton, feathers and fur. There are a number of different kinds of clothes moth, but the majority of damage can be put down to the common clothes moth. As with that other creepy vandal the woodworm, cleanliness can be a great discouragement. It is the grubs that do the mischief, hatching out from the eggs the lady moth will have laid in some fold or hem suitably decorated and rendered attractive by a little neglected dirt. She is careless with her eggs and they are not attached by any goo when they are laid, so they can be shaken out. But this is not always the best procedure as you can never be sure where they have fallen, and it is in this way quite possible to spread the infestation. Better to go on a systematic egg or grub hunt. When found, brush out carefully into a container. If the fabric is sound and colours fast the pieces suspected of contamination may be immersed in water at a temperature of 60°C (140°F). Ten seconds of this will murder both eggs and grubs.

There is also the carpet beetle, a nasty little thing that can find what it thinks is a cosy home in a shaggy Turkey carpet or an Axminster, but only if the carpet has been neglected and become comfortable for him with dirt. Pretty well all these brethren of destruction revel in dirt, so keep the brush and cleaner in use. To get rid of this pest it is probably better to use a dry proprietary powder preparation in preference to a liquid type, as the latter might effect the dyes. Sprinkle on the powder following the instructions on the container and leave for about eight hours and then take off with a vacuum cleaner. For other discouragements see the following heading.

### Insect repellents

There are a number of commercial proprietary products available for use to protect textiles from attack by pests. These come in liquid, atomised spray, powder or solid form. Generally they should not be allowed to come in contact with the actual fabrics. They are often quite highly toxic and dangerous and not in the least desirable to have around the home. If you must use them, follow the instructions on the container.

Is there an alternative? Yes. Reach for a sound book on herbs. Traditional methods can still be as effective today as they were in the past. Aromatic oils such as spike, better known as lavender, can be quite efficacious on their own and when spike is mixed with citronella you make a sweet-smelling perfume that sends many insect nasties weeping all the way home. In fact I have seen at a picnic alongside the Loire a mean-minded hornet go into a full power-dive at an unsuspecting girl. The hornet got within striking range, caught the aromatic vapours of spike and citronella she was wearing and hit his air-brakes hard, executed a sharp U turn and was gone. Spike and citronella are obtainable from a chemist and most of the herbs *etc* mentioned here are available from a herbalist.

Other plants that are waiting just to help you with pest problems include: crushed columbine seeds, eucalyptus leaves, pennyroyal oil, garlic (if you are that kind of family), laurel leaves, mugwort, pine needles, red cedar wood, rue, sweet flag root, tansy, winter savory, wormwood and yellow meliot. Why not a pot-pourri of some of the more fragrant of these to place in a wardrobe, or some pomanders to hang about the place, or some sachets containing dried herbs to protect items put away in drawers? Other plants ready to be recruited into this scheme for pest removal, which can be made up into sprays or dusting powders, include alder bark, aniseed, derris root, feverfew, hellebore root, larkspur seed, juniper, pyrethrum flowers, thyme oil, and several of those listed above. Last word: whatever deterrent is chosen, keep it away from close contact with any fabrics.

## Ironing
From the presentation point of view this is very often desirable. Always inspect thoroughly any suspect age-old items, as if fibres are weakened already, a hot iron is not going to help. Frail objects can be laid flat between sheets of tissue or blotting paper and put in a linen press if available or, failing that, with some pieces of wood or hardboard on top and some heavy weight holding them down.

If an iron is used, always use one with an adjustable heat control, and play for safety by using it one setting under what it indicates for a particular type of material. With fabrics that are stained and earmarked for treatment, never iron until the stain has been removed because the heat can often help to fix the mark still more firmly.

## Lace and crochet
Both these materials can be dry cleaned as described above and they can also be washed in a tray. But in both cases they should be supported on a piece of fine net or plastic sheet when being

put into the tray and also when being lifted out. After treatment they should be smoothed out to their correct shape on a firm support and if necessary fixed in position using non-rusting pins. A partial drying can be carried out first by placing the lace between two sheets of clean white blotting paper.

For frail examples, or pieces mounted on pillows or with upholstery, use potato flour as suggested under *Embroidery*. A second course can be to spoon out a liberal amount of powdered French chalk over the grime and smudgy marks. Work this well in with the fingertips and then brush off and repeat if necessary.

For exceptionally fragile pieces a strengthening treatment can be given by lightly spraying the backs with a solution of weak starch or a mixture of one part acrylic medium and four parts water. When storing lace, always roll it round small wads of tissue paper rather than folding it.

## Light hazards

Both daylight and artificial light, whether tungsten or fluorescent, will have a destructive effect on textiles. Strong light combined with excessive humidity can wreak quite astonishing damage on seemingly sound fabrics. Not only will colours fade dramatically but also fibres will weaken and even finally break down. Over-lighting does not really mean better visibility and enjoyment of your treasures. Where possible, screen from, or move out of, direct sunlight. (See INTRODUCTION for advice on protection from ultra-violet rays.)

## Stain removal, general hints

Textiles seem to draw stains to themselves, particularly with upholstery, table linen and costumes, and also carpets and rugs. The removal of these marks may not always be easy and can put the material at risk unless you are very careful. Stains can cause fabrics to rot and they can combine with elements of the materials. They may be absorbed into the material. They can build up in flat lumps embedded into the weave, but will not actually stain the fibres; or they may be a combination of all three types. The main snag with old marks is that it may be near to impossible to be sure just what they were made by. Careful examination and comparison with other examples known to you may narrow the choice. Then it will be a matter for careful and minute trials with weak solvents and chemicals that are mentioned below.

Some general rules to remember when treating stains with liquids:

1 Always take tests for colour fastness.

2 Always start with a circle of weak cleaning liquid and work towards the centre, so as to avoid a ring mark forming.

3 Use distilled water whenever water is mentioned in a remedy, when dealing with valuable old pieces.

4 Test out even the weakest bleaches on any material on which they may be used.

The list of stains below is by no means a full one but it deals with those most likely to be found. There are many proprietary stain removers around and most should be harmless if used as per the instructions on the container. Take a second glance at one if it states it will remove every known stain. It probably will – and the fabric as well.

A general plan should be, wherever possible, to put a piece of white blotting paper, clean white rag or a pad of paper tissues underneath the stain when it is being worked on. Be patient with an obstinate one and resist the temptation to treble or quadruple the strength of any suggested remedy; almost certainly damage will come this way. Several weak applications are far better. Work near a window to assist drying; a hair dryer is handy in case an accelerated drying is needed.

*Warning*: make sure ventilation is adequate if toxic chemicals are being used. Protect hands with rubber gloves or barrier cream if materials to be used indicate such a course.

## Stains, types of

*Acids*
Where possible these should be dealt with at the double. Course one can be to sponge with a solution of 25 g (1 oz) of borax or washing soda in 600 ml (1 pint) of warm water, then rinse thoroughly. Course two, if colours are fast, 15 ml (1 tbsp) of ammonia with 600 ml (1 pint) of warm water. Three, especially for carpets, use a saturated solution of bicarbonate of soda in warm water, sponge and rinse. If colours are fast, the ammonia solution can be used. Emergency first aid can be given with a bottle or syphon of soda water.

## Adhesives
*Animal and fish glues* Working at them with warm water will win through; don't try fancy chemicals with these.

*Contacts and instants* These will probably need acetone, but thorough warming with hand-hot water will help the action.

*Epoxies* Acetone again, warm water treatment can only help.

## Alcohol
Generally clean water will do the necessary if a stain is caught whilst still damp; if not, use a mild detergent with warm water and work in with fingertips or a not too hard scrubbing brush. Rinse and leave to dry, if possible with a wad of something underneath to increase ventilation.

## Alkalis
Mop with cotton wool and a weak mixture of white vinegar and water, then rinse by swabbing with water.

## Beer
This strangely enough seldom leaves a stain. If one does appear, wash or sponge it with warm soapy water that contains a little ammonia or white vinegar. On white materials a weak bleach of one part 20 vol. hydrogen peroxide to six parts water may be used and then rinsed off.

## Beetroot
Use 25 g (1 oz) of borax to 600 ml (1 pint) of warm water, either directly on to the stain, or by placing stained area over the top of a jug and pouring the solution through the material.

## Bird droppings
The borax solution above should do most of the work. A gentle bleaching with 20 vol. hydrogen peroxide one part to six parts water or a 2% solution of Chloramine T, obtainable from a chemist (see GLOSSARY). Rinse well.

## Blacklead
This often drifts across on to a fireside rug or carpet. It should come away with white spirit.

### Blood

Almost the worst stain there is, especially if of an early vintage; in fact with some really early drops it is probably better to leave them as the rigorous treatments required may easily damage the fabric.

For comparatively fresh blood stains the treatment can start by sponging with cold salt water. This may be followed by the application of a light bleach, using 2% Chloramine T; rinse and follow with 2% oxalic acid (*warning*: highly poisonous). Rinse several times.

### Candle wax

Put clean white blotting paper or brown wrapping paper each side. Apply a reasonably hot iron, the temperature depending on the fabric being treated. Keep replacing the blotting or wrapping papers until the mark has nearly gone, then remove final traces with white spirit. If on upholstery you will just have to have the paper on the top side.

### Chewing gum

Egg white worked in should soften the nasty mess so that most can be picked off and the rest sponged away with warm soapy water. Second shot, chill well with ice and pick off, then if colour fast wash away remnants, or use proprietary aerosol (see PRO-DUCTS).

### Chocolate

Scrape off what you can with the back edge of a knife or plastic spatula and attack with warm soapy water plus borax, as for *Beet-root*. On white materials, bleach out residual marks with weak hydrogen peroxide or 2% Chloramine T (see GLOSSARY) and rinse well.

### Coffee

If caught fresh it may be sponged out with the borax solution recommended for *Beetroot* followed by washing with warm soapy water and rinsing. Alternatively, put fabric over the top of a jug and pour borax solution through, or really hot water depending on material. Old obstinate stains can be rubbed with glycerine and left for about an hour, rinsed out and washed with warm soapy water. Small spot marks if still fresh will often shift if blotting paper is put both sides and they are given a light quick touch with a hot iron.

## Cosmetics

Lipstick will sometimes shift with just warm soapy water, but if not, rub into the stain vaseline or glycerine and wash with warm soapy water with a little ammonia. Foundation creams and their like should be treated by leaving a little potato flour (obtainable from a grocery or chemist) over them for about an hour, brush this off, and wash. If fabrics cannot be washed, use heated potato flour (see *Embroidery*, page 95).

## Cream

See *Cosmetics* above.

## Creosote

This shouldn't really get into a house but someone can walk through with a dribbling tin. Place a wad of rag underneath and work away at the mark, starting with a piece of lard or butter and massaging it in with the fingertips; oils such as eucalyptus or lavender may also be tried. Rinse out with white spirit and then wash with warm soapy water, rinse and dry.

## Curry

Caught quickly, it should come right away with a mild borax treatment (see *Beetroot*) followed by warm soapy water. On whites, one of the previously mentioned gentle bleaches such as Chloramine T may be used, followed by a thorough rinse.

## Egg

Remove as much as you can with a plastic spatula or similar blunt edge. Egg white should loosen with salt and water. Egg yolk can be tougher but should break down with a mild solution of an enzyme detergent worked into it with the back of a wooden spoon, then wash with warm soapy water.

## Fats and oils

Depending on their thickness there are two ways to break them up. If thick, treat as for *Candle wax*; if fairly thin, dab with white spirit. In both cases, finish by washing and a thorough rinsing.

## Fruit juices in general

If caught whilst still moist, place material over the top of a jug and pour very hot water through the mark from a height. If the stain is obstinate, dab with lemon juice and wash. With a dried-out stain, use the borax solution (see *Beetroot*). If a real sticker, apply a 2% solution of Chloramine T bleach, rinse, follow up with 2% oxalic acid (*warning*: highly poisonous) and rinse several times. Some-times a little ammonia with warm soapy water may be effective. For fabrics that cannot be washed by their nature or position, sponge any marks with cold water then work in a little glycerine with fingertips, leave for half an hour, sponge out and dab with a little white vinegar; rinse.

## Grass
If normal washing does not remove, dab with a little methylated spirits; eucalyptus oil can help. For woollen materials use equal amounts of tartaric acid (cream of tartar) and salt mixed to a paste with water. Leave on for about five minutes, wash off and rinse well.

## Hygiene, lack of
Sponge areas with warm solution of borax or bicarbonate of soda, 50 g (2 oz) to 600 ml (1 pint) of water. Where possible place rag pads underneath before starting. Rinse well. Then wash with warm soapy water, again rinse, finish with a light application of some pleasant but effective disinfectant.

## Indelible pencil
If material is suitable, dab with a little acetone or methylated spirits. White fabrics can be bleached with weak hydrogen peroxide or 2% solution of Chloramine T. Rinse well.

## Ink
*Ballpoint ink* This can be one of the most stubborn stains. Some will come away with methylated spirits. Others may need some-thing of the order of petroleum ether (highly inflammable). Don't be tempted into using carbon tetrachloride, as both the liquid and the fumes are poisonous. Proprietary liquids are available, but try to find out if they contain carbon tetrachloride and if so put them back on the shelf.

*Felt-tip ink* Methylated spirits should take out the ink of most brands of felt-tip pens; follow through with washing. If on white materials further treatment is needed, finish with a light bleaching and thorough rinsing.

*Fountain-pen ink* Reduce stain as far as possible by dabbing with warm water. Make a paste of a little salt with lemon juice and place over stain for ten minutes and try sluicing away; if still obstinate, repeat treatment. On wool or silk a 2% solution of hydrochloric acid made up by your chemist may be tried; on cotton or linen 2% Chloramine T. Rinse well in both these cases.

*Indian ink* This is likely to be based on shellac and so should loosen with methylated spirits.

*Marking ink* The two most common kinds are based either on an aniline black dye or on silver nitrate. Both of them can be really tenacious. Work first with a 2% Chloramine T bleach solution, rinse off with distilled water, then a 2% oxalic acid solution prepared by your chemist; again rinse off well with distilled water. If that fails, try again with the oxalic acid solution heated to hand warmth. The third attempt can be to leave the item soaking overnight in distilled water and then apply the bleach and oxalic acid treatment the next day.

*Warning*: oxalic acid is highly poisonous.

*Red ink* Fresh stains should come away with a weak solution of borax and water. Old stains may respond to methylated spirits with the addition of a little white vinegar; if not, use a 2% oxalic acid solution (*warning*: highly poisonous). Rinse well in all cases.

## Iodine
Sponge with warm soapy water with a little ammonia. Second choice is hypo, used for developing and printing by photographers and available from a chemist or photographic supply shop. This should take it out rapidly; rinse well.

## Iron mould
One of the nasty ones and sadly quite common. It will atack pretty well all materials with obvious orange-brown rust stains. Get your chemist to make up a 2% solution of oxalic acid and distilled water, and mix up a 2% solution of Chloramine T, again with distilled water. You should also have a bowl of distilled water to hand. Place a rag or piece of blotting paper under the mark and dab on the Chloramine T, leave for about a minute, rinse off with the distilled water, apply the oxalic acid solution, leave for about a minute and rinse thoroughly with distilled water. Blot and spread out to dry. The procedure can be repeated if needed to clear residual spots, or the order of application reversed.

To my knowledge this somewhat drastic treatment has been carried out on an old Chinese silk brocade blouse; some ten years later there are no signs of any deterioration.

Other less venturesome alternatives can be a paste of lemon juice and salt left on for an hour and then thoroughly rinsed, or the use of a proprietary rust stain remover (see PRODUCTS). Some have faith in an infusion of old rhubarb leaves (back to oxalic acid).

*Warning*: oxalic acid is a potent poison, whatever the source.

### Jams and marmalades
Scrape off with a plastic spatula, and sponge the area with warm soapy water; if there are residual marks sponge with weak borax solution (see *Beetroot*) and rinse well.

### Lead pencil
If the material is firm, stiffened or starched, a soft eraser or piece of art gum should remove most of the marks; sponge off remaining marks with warm soapy water and rinse. On whites, traces can be bleached out with a 2% solution of Chloramine T; rinse well.

### Metal polishes
Never neglect, particularly with carpets, or these polishes can produce a lasting blemish. Sponge off with warm soapy water as soon as possible and rinse several times with well-moistened cloths.

### Mildew
There are good proprietary liquids for the treatment of this despoiling stain. For old-established marks the 2% Chloramine T and 2% oxalic acid treatment described under *Ink* (*Marking*) should remove all traces. If these marks do appear it is a warning that the source should be looked for. It is probable that there is some place where your fabrics are stored that has a stagnant rather damp area.

### Milk
Spillages should never be just given a cursory wipe over with a damp rag. If left, they can go rancid and bring in train unpleasant troubles. Wash first with warm soapy water; if some staining is still evident, repeat but add some borax to the water. If rich milk, it might be best to start with white spirit to dissolve most of the fats. If marks persist on whites, a little gentle bleach can be used with safety.

### Nail varnish
This stain will almost certainly need acetone, although methylated spirits could be tried first.

### Paints
*Acrylics* If caught moist these will come off with water; if hardened, leave a pad of cotton wool soaked in methylated spirits over stain for about ten minutes. By that time the acrylic should have loosened enough to wash away.

*Alkyds* Follow the treatment for oils, given below.

*Egg tempera* If still moist this will come away with water; if set, it can be very obstinate. The area of the marks could be gently crumpled through the finger and thumb to break up the paint film. Then wash with warm water and a little gentle detergent and agitate the paint marks with a fairly stiff artist's paint brush. Wash the stained area again and rinse.

*Emulsion* (household) Use methylated spirits.

*Oil colours* If still moist these will come away with white spirit. If hardened, there will be trouble. A very gentle dab of paint stripper will be needed; wearing gloves, put this on with a cotton bud and as soon as there is any sign of the paint wrinkling, stop the action of the stripper with white spirit and work at the residue with a small brush. Finally, give the hard worked fabric a well-earned rinsing with warm soapy water and warm clear water.

### Perspiration
Dab with a swab moistened with a solution of 1 part white vinegar to 16 parts warm water. Second attempt: dab with a very weak solution of ammonia. Third attempt: sponge lightly with methylated spirits. Residual marks can be bleached out with 2% Chloramine T solution and well rinsed.

### Plasticine
An obstinate mess if clogged in wool or other heavy materials. Scrape off what you can and then use one or other of the proprietary cleaners (see PRODUCTS) that will handle this.

### Rust
In many ways quite close to Iron mould (see above). It can be spotted out with a small paint brush using increasing strengths of hydrogen peroxide. Rinse well afterwards. A 2% oxalic acid

solution (*warning*: highly poisonous) may also be tried, again rinsing well.

## Scorching

Washing over with a warm solution of 50 g (2 oz) of borax to 600 ml (1 pint) of water can do much to reduce the marks. This could be followed by gentle bleaching if the materials will stand it. Some advocate dabbing on a little dilute citric acid and leaving out in the sun to bring on a bleaching. Severe scorching can sometimes be successfully reduced by mixing up a paste of borax and glycerine which is then spread thickly over the mark. Leave on overnight and then wash and rinse normally. Residual marks on whites may be bleached clear. Back to the vegetable garden, one voice told me that a fresh scorch can be taken out by rubbing with a newly cut onion then giving a good soaking in cold water.

## Sealing wax

Crumble off as much of the surplus wax as possible; and then place clean blotting paper each side of the residue and apply a hot iron. Sponge off the remains with methylated spirits and wash and rinse.

## Shoe polish

A little gentle rubbing with a swab of cotton wool moistened with white spirit should remove the marks without trouble.

## Soot

This is liable to get into a rug or carpet after a fall of soot from a chimney during a gale. Take off what you can with a vacuum cleaner. Then sprinkle thickly a powder such as potato flour, talcum powder, starch or French chalk over the marked area. Work this into the pile until it is dirty, repeat if needed two or three times. Vacuum off and give a surface wipe with a cloth dipped in warm soapy water followed by one dipped in plain water; leave to dry.

## Tar

Scrape off excess with a plastic spatula or similar blunt-edged instrument and swab the area with a piece of cotton wool dipped in white spirit, turpentine or eucalyptus oil. Hard residual marks can be softened with glycerine or olive oil and then cleared with white spirit. Wash with a solution of detergent and water and give several rinses.

*Tea*

If still wet, place marked fabric over the top of a jug and pour hot water from a height through the material. Dried stains can be tackled with a borax solution: one part borax to 30 parts water. On woollen materials a gentle bleach of one part of 20 vol. hydrogen peroxide to 6 parts of water may be tried, rinsing well afterwards.

*Urine and other animal stains*
See *Hygiene, lack of*

*Wine*

If still damp, stretch material over the top of a jug and pour hot water from a height through the fabric. Marks if dried out can be sponged with a weak solution of borax and water, repeat using increasing strengths, then wash well with warm soapy water and thoroughly rinse. Dry stains may also be softened up by applying glycerine leaving for a few minutes and then washing out. Wine stains on upholstery should be dabbed with cotton wool as soon as possible to remove excess. Then the area should be sprinkled fairly thickly with potato flour, talcum or French chalk. Knead this in and as it becomes tacky, remove and repeat; finally swab with cotton wool dipped in glycerine, leave a few minutes, sponge with warm soapy water and rinse with wrung-out cloths.

## Tapestries

Often by their somewhat rough texture tapestries will tend to gather dust from the atmosphere. They will very likely be of some age and may easily be fragile and should never be given any home liquid treatments. Always consult an expert. Surface dust can be safely removed by gently passing a soft cloth pad over the tapestry following the main grain lines. Don't fall for suggestions that such and such a liquid will brighten up the colours. It may do and it may also do irreversible damage to the delicate tints and beautiful materials.

## Tears and fraying

If possible these should always be attended to from the back of the material. On upholstery this may not always be possible, thus wefts and warps should be sorted out so that they lie in their original intended positions. Then with threads, silks, cottons, wools matched as close in tint and thickness as possible, darn in to simulate the existing pattern. Where a delicate area has been ripped, attach a piece of fine nylon net behind to give support, at the same time as doing the darning. Some fragile materials may also be strengthened with weak starch on the reverse side; but if this does not suit the nature of the material, an acrylic dressing with its flexible film will be better. Prepare a mixture of one part acrylic matt medium (obtainable from an art shop) to three parts of water. This may then be applied to the back of the fabric by an atomising spray or carefully brushed over the surface where it is needed.

Be very cautious about touching any embroidery or lace of value; unless you are a highly skilled needle hand, pass it to one who is and will have the necessary knowledge of whatever method has been used.

## Washing techniques

Any fabrics selected for washing should be carefully examined for signs of frailty and tests for colour fastness should be made.

Washing should be where possible in soft water and in as large a sink or bath as available; be sure that there are no sharp edges or obstructions that could cause damage. The flatter the internal base of the container the better; run plain cold water in to start with to a depth sufficient to submerge the fabric to be washed. Place the piece to be cleaned on a support of net or plastic sheet, pick up the support and lower into the water. Gently knead all over with the fingertips and then leave to soak for around half an hour, changing the water two or three times.

Lift the fabric out, empty bath and refill with warm water and add a small amount of mild soap flakes or quality liquid soap. Lower the fabric back into the bath and continue kneading all over with patient and gentle fingertips. Lastly, lift out and empty off dirty water, refill with clean warm water, replace fabric and give gentle but thorough rinsing in at least three waters. When rinsing water is quite clear, lift, drain and gently slide off support material on to a firm table-top or similar surface and arrange in natural position. Dab off what excess moisture you can with towelling and leave to dry; this may be accelerated by the use of a hair-dryer.

### *Specially delicate fabrics*

Fabrics that are delicate or which have to be washed in position, are often best treated with a solution of saponin, a derivative from the soapwort plant. This gentle but effective cleaner should be mixed with a little warm water and then lightly brushed into the area. The resulting foam should be lifted off with a cloth, and the fabric rinsed by dabbing with a moist cloth or piece of cotton wool. Saponin extract is obtainable as a white powder or can be prepared yourself.

There are quite a number of plants that contain compounds called saponins in sufficient quantities to produce a froth when beaten up in water. The resulting liquid can be strained and may be used for a shampoo for many textiles, and it will be gentle and unlikely to leave any residual undesirable scums. These soapy plants include Amole root, California soap plant root, California soap root bulb, guaiac leaves, papaya leaves, quillai bark, red campion leaves and roots, saltbush root, soapberry fruit, soap pod fruit, soap tree, yucca root, soapwort root, Spanish bayonet root. Some textile restorers are exploring the possibilities of these natural agents, and inquiries at a herbalist could help in tracking them down.

Another treatment for a small delicate piece of fabric can be to put it into a large mouthed 10l (2 gal) glass jar. Fill with warm water and add about 150 g (5 oz) of mild soap flakes. Now gently rock the jar for about five minutes. Pour off the washing water, holding a hand over the mouth of the jar and letting the liquid strain through the fingers. Refill with cold water and rock again to rinse; repeat this two or three times, then empty out water, remove fabric and spread out on a firm surface, easing to correct shape and leave to dry.

If a piece of fabric has an overall slightly stained look, it can be soaked overnight in a mild solution of sodium perborate (one part to 300), then rinsed out thoroughly and washed in the normal way.

# Leathers

Our use of skins goes way back to somewhere during the Palaeolithic period. Just when is not completely certain, but there are wall paintings of the Upper Palaeolithic times, which date from about 75,000 to 10,000 BC, in the caves Els Secans near Mazaleon, and Teruel and Cogul near Lerida, Spain, and which show human figures disporting themselves in what are quite evidently skin skirts and trousers. Those early skin-workers left behind tools of their trade: skin scrapers used for removing the surplus flesh and hair have been found. Their preparation of the skins probably went no further than sun-drying and perhaps rubbing in brains and fat to try to keep the skins supple. The early Egyptians produced tawed leather, skins that had been treated with salt or alum, the product being a stiff white material. In the tomb of Rekhmire, Thebes, dating from around 1450 BC, is a scene showing Egyptian leather-dressers at work, covering a shield with a skin, treating a panther's skin in a jar of some preparation and cutting up a skin with a half-moon knife.

For tanning, the Middle Eastern craftsmen used oak-galls (an excrescence produced on some species of oak, caused by the puncture of a gallfly); Egyptians worked a mixture of alum and oil into leather for sandals; other leathers might be 'fed' with substances such as grease, egg-yolk, flour and various oils. A wide variety of plants and trees supplied the raw materials for the essential tanning, where briefly what happens is that the tannic acid combines with the protein of the hide to give it resistance to decay. During the centuries, such as these have been used: black alder bark, black wattle bark, Douglas fir bark, dwarf sumach leaves, hemlock spruce bark, Iceland moss and tanner's dock root. Leather-workers on the search for softer and finer leathers have at times gone in for rather grotesque processes; just think of my fine early Renaissance lady attending some great function with the Medicis, on her feet beautiful soft leather shoes that had been given their supple quality by soaking the leather in a cold infusion of poultry or pigeon droppings or with a warm infusion of dog-dung. Such can be the demands of fashion.

Leather has been used, apart from footwear, for numerous purposes: for armour fittings, large vessels known as black jacks for ale made from tarred leather, hanging bottles known as costrels, gloves, coverings for chests, chair seats and backs, baggage, hosepipes, harness, bookbindings, screens, wall hangings and upholstery. Some artists have even used it as a support for painting on. In the National Gallery of Art, Washington DC, there is a ceremonial shield of leather on which Andrea del Castagno (*c* 1423–*c* 57) painted *The Young David*. The skins of many animals have been employed, for example: cattle, deer, goats, horses and pigs as well as those from reptiles, some birds, and with bookbinding, human.

---

## Some types of leather

*Calfskin*
Popular for bookbinding; soft and smooth with a lack of grain, calfskin works well with dyes and other decorative treatments.

*Chamois*
Originally prepared from the skin of the chamois, an antelope from the Alps and Pyrenees. Now more often made from skins from sheep, goats and deer. Sometimes used in upholstery.

*Levant*
A kind of morocco that has large and irregular graining, much used for top quality bookbinding.

*Mocha*
Fine soft leather from the skin of an Arabian goat.

*Morocco*
Fine leather, the best of which generally comes from France, Switzerland and Turkey. From goatskin which has been tanned with sumach and dyed on the grain side; it may have been first developed by the Moors. Imitation morocco is made from sheepskin and known in the trade as 'roan'; it is largely used for upholstery and bookbinding.

*Shagreen*
Skins from certain species of the ray family of fish and sharks

that after being treated have been used to cover tea caddies, knife cases, telescope barrels, etc. Imitation shagreens are made by pressing small seeds into the outside of horse skins whilst they are still moist; this simulates the characteristic graining of the genuine article.

The early vegetable-tanned leathers appear to have a far greater lasting power than those of today. Leather by its nature is prone to attack from atmospheric conditions, and thus should be kept adequately protected. Near correct relative humidity, *ie,* around 65%, is important to avoid mould growths from excess dampness or, at the other end of the scale, deterioration from excess dryness. Air pollutants, especially from industrial and urban areas, can carry chemicals which will be destructive to leather. In the remains of rotted bookbindings there are nearly always traces of sulphuric acid. Under attack by sulphur dioxide and other such chemical substances, leather can develop the so-called 'red rot'; this brings on a corrosion that starts the deterioration of the fibrous structure and if no measures are taken the leather finally disintegrates into red dust. But with due care and the use of the right materials much can be done to save the leather objects we collect and use.

## Problems, products and processes

### Cleaning
Before doing anything, thoroughly examine the leather for signs of insect attack (see *Insect pests*), deterioration and damage. If any of these are present they should be dealt with first. Again if the object is of value, pass the job along to an expert.

If the piece is sound and just grimy, first of all, with a soft cloth, get rid of all dry dirt. Then it is permissible to wipe over the surface with a swab of cotton wool that has been dipped into a mild soap and water solution and well squeezed out; do not make the leather in any way wet or even damp. Wipe over with a second swab dipped just in water and again well squeezed out. Dry with more cotton wool or some towelling. Saddle soap is a good cleaner, and this is best applied with a small sponge. Work up a lather and remove this with a second clean, nearly dry, sponge and when dry finish with a clean soft cloth.

There are a number of proprietary leather cleaners which can be helpful, but study their instructions and note, if possible, constituents. Any use of harsh solvents could be harmful, as they can penetrate the leather and remove natural substances helping to hold the fibres together.

In the PRODUCTS section at the end of the book some preparations are suggested that will be found to bring back a life and substance; there is also the well-tried and successful British Museum Leather Dressing which is quite simple to make up. Your local chemist will be able to get the ingredients.

*200 g (7 oz) anhydrous lanolin*
*15 g (¹/2 oz) beeswax*
*30 ml (1 fl oz) cedarwood oil*
*312 ml (11 fl oz) hexane (highly inflammable)*

Put the hexane into a bottle large enough to hold all the ingredients, then break up the beeswax into small chips and add to the hexane and shake until completely dissolved. Next add the lanolin, shake again and put in the cedarwood oil. When using always keep it well shaken up.

*Warning*: fire precautions needed; do not smoke or work near a naked flame.

This and other dressings mentioned in PRODUCTS can often work wonders. The dressing will clean, feed the starved leather, bring up colour and give a foundation for future polishing. It should be applied sparsely with a piece of cotton wool and then left for about 48 hours. After this time the surfaces can be buffed up with more cotton wool or a really soft cloth. If the dressing is being applied to areas such as the spines of leatherbound books or where there is dry fraying and deterioration, the moistened swabs should be gently dabbed on rather than wiped over the surface. For excessively dried out areas a second application can be given after about a week.

## Consolidation

Leather has appeared in strange forms as worked by some craftsmen of old. Examples of decorated frames modelled from leather may be found, and also plaques with small modelled portrait busts. Objects such as these may have become very fragile and can need some form of impregnation to support them. There are polyacrylate resin preparations (see WHERE TO GET WHAT) that can be applied simply and successfully with a soft brush. If the immediate surface has some firmness the liquid can be gently but liberally applied over both sides and edges of the object. If it is only possible to get at the front because the piece is mounted on wood, take a hypodermic syringe and delicately inject the fluid. The leather is liable to darken as the fluid is brushed on or injected but this will be only temporary and will disappear as the solvent carrying the resin evaporates. Be quite sure that the leather is absolutely dry before starting, and if the leather has been dyed or in any other way coloured, take a fastness test first.

*Warning*: these applications should only be used where there is adequate ventilation.

## Desk tops

These often give cause for concern. An 18th-century desk with a leather top may be in excellent condition except for the top which can look downright miserable, faded, scuffed and stained. If a new top is put on, however fine an example, it - well, it just *looks* new and out of harmony with the soft gleam of the sur-rounding wood. Give that skin from the 18th century all the help you can.

Generally round the edges the leather will be coming loose. First step, working carefully, is to remove as much of the old glue as possible. Lay back the areas that have come free over a piece of cardboard and ease off this original adhesive with a sharp knife or scalpel. At the same time scrape away the remains of glue from the underlying wood. The glue the original craftsman used was probably a hoof or rabbit-skin. One of these may be used for the repair but if this is done, be careful not to get the leather too damp as this can make it buckle and so it will be dif-ficult to get down flat. There are proprietary adhesives tailored for this kind of join, leather to wood. They will more than likely have a plasticiser among their ingredients which can take care of any slight movement by the leather later.

### Restoring the tooling

If there have been simple ruled gold border lines and they have been rubbed away, it is not too difficult to replace them, using a small leather tooling wheel (obtainable from some artists' supply stores). At the same time, buy some gold transfer tape. Lay this tape along the direction of the line and run the wheel, which has previously been heated, along a ruler and over the surface of the transfer tape (*see diagram 11a*). Do not overheat the wheel or the leather will be scorched. After this, peel off the paper backing of the transfer tape (*see diagram 11b*), and with a soft-hair brush remove any surplus gold. The tooling wheel can also be used for

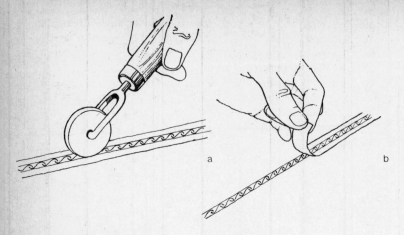

*Diagram IIa, b  Restoring tooling on a leather desk top*

'blind' tool lines that can afterwards be partially filled with a little wax polish and pigment to match the original blind tooled lines.

When any reattachment has hardened off the whole surface of the leather top can be treated with the dressing mentioned above under *Cleaning*, or with a proprietary brand. Do not put anything back on to the surface for at least four days, preferably longer.

### Fungal attack

Under damp and stagnant air conditions leather is liable to fungal attacks, and these may cause staining or a change of colour in dyed leathers. This menace is best defeated by ventilation, which will remove the most encouraging cause of its growth. In damp climates it will probably be necessary to apply a fungicide. One of the most reliable is paranitrophenol, but this can cause yellow staining; if diluted, however, with distilled water or alcohol to a strength of 0.35%, staining will be very slight and is acceptable. A second fungicide is pentachlorophenol, which may also be diluted with distilled water or alcohol down to a strength of 0.25%. Either of these could be made up for you by a chemist.

Another way to discourage the organisms that cause fungal attack can be to give a light atomised spraying of thymol as a saturated solution in alcohol; this could also be sprayed over shelves and the backs of bookcases where volumes are likely to be affected, and inside objects such as black jacks that are for display and not for domestic use.

## Gilding

Where this has been used decoratively with leather it may have become dimmed by layers of wax polish or surface grime. These decorations can be brought up by touching very carefully with a minute swab of cotton wool dipped in white spirit. When doing this, have another dry piece of cotton wool in the other hand, and follow right along behind the white spirit, swab – drying up at once. The same kind of application can be made, using a weak ammonia solution; this time, though, follow up with a swab moistened with water to rinse and then dry. Make every effort to keep both cleaners off the surrounding leather.

## Heat and light hazards

As far as possible, keep all leather objects well away from direct heat sources and avoid putting leatherbound books on shelves over radiators. Prolonged exposure to excessive heat will seriously desiccate the body of the leather.

Direct sunlight will also cause desiccation, and probably fading. Watch that display lights are not so close that they can cause overheating.

## Insect pests

Leather is palatable to moth grubs and also other parasites that can chew their way into and through objects, particularly book bindings. If the infestation is caught early on and there are only a few books involved you can fumigate these yourself. Line a large biscuit or similar tin with clean white paper, arrange the books opened out fan-wise and have a small wide-mouthed jar with about 50 g (2 oz) of dichlorobenzene crystals per 28 l (1 cu ft). Seal lid of the tin with Sellotape and leave for at least a week. If the marauders should be around they can be discouraged by giving leather objects a light application of a good wax polish that contains a safe insecticide. Book shelves should be given a light atomised spray with a fluid domestic insecticide to frighten off these pests.

## Polishing

Select a proprietary preparation that states it is suitable for leather (see PRODUCTS). The beeswax polish recommended for furniture (see page 21) when made up to a fairly thin cream will serve with most leather objects, but as it may leave a minimal tackiness with books it is better to use a good white polish made from a different basis. Whatever polish is chosen, it should be applied sparingly, left for about half an hour and then buffed up with cotton wool or a soft cloth. For some objects, a sufficient polish will be given by buffing up two days after the application of the dressing mentioned above under *Cleaning*.

## Repairs

Repairs should always be carried out before any dressing or polish is applied, as these can prevent adhesives taking properly. Previously applied polish can be largely removed with methylated spirits or white spirit; let whichever has been used evaporate thoroughly before making a start. Try to keep the application of the solvents to the immediate areas of the damage, as they may take out the tanning substances. Where there are actually fragments missing, small patches can be cut from a piece of like leather and sanded down so that they are the same thickness as that being repaired. The edges can be bevelled to assist fitting. When sticking leather to leather it is important to choose an adhesive that is specifically for this material. Apart from adequate sticking power it should have a plasticiser to allow for tiny movements of the leather. With small repairs it should be possible to match up colours of the leather with tinted polishes or dyes.

### Restoring a leather screen

Leather screens can often give trouble because of the uses for which they are intended. They spend their lives shielding us from either cold draughts or excessive heat from fireplaces, and often as well they are expected to provide shade from an over-strong July sun streaming in through south facing windows. They can be brutes to deal with, and if they are of rarity and value, pass them straight down to a craftsman's workshop. But if they are of fairly recent date and of no great worth other than for utilitarian purposes and you have time and a large table, have a try. The main troubles will be splitting, desiccation, possibly some rotting, painted decoration flaking or peeling and mould stains.

1 Dismount the leather from the leaves of the screen, one leaf at a time, supporting the panel carefully as it comes away and lay it face down on a piece of clean cloth on the table.

2 Remove old backing such as linen, muslin or scrim and also as much of the old glue as you can.

3 Relax the leather (essential if it is brittle and buckling) as fol-

lows: slide the panel off the cloth on to a sheet of glass or heavy vinyl sheeting and damp the leather down fairly thoroughly with an atomised water spray; allow to penetrate. Cover with a thin sheet of plastic and place on top a sheet of hardboard or chipboard and then weight this down with any handy heavy objects, trying to get an even distribution.

**4** Leave the above for about two days, meanwhile preparing a wooden stretcher frame that is about 7 cm (3 in) bigger all round than that of the screen leaf (*see diagram 12a*).

**5** Lift off the weights, the hardboard or chipboard and the plastic sheet; allow 24 hours for any excess moisture to dry away.

**6** Slide panel off vinyl or glass, still face down, on to a sheet of plastic, and be sure that this will not accept the adhesive.

**7** On the prepared stretcher, loosely staple-stretch a piece of medium quality unprimed artist's canvas (*see diagram 12a*).

**8** Give the canvas a thin coat of a leather adhesive that will also 'take' on textiles, and also apply a coat to the back of the leather; allow a few minutes for these to go tacky.

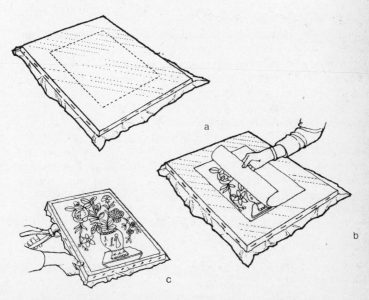

*Diagram 12a, b, c Restoring a leather screen*

**9** Bring canvas and leather together, turn frame face down and apply even pressure to the back of the canvas with a rubber roller.

**10** Turn the stretcher and panel over, peel off the plastic protective sheet (*see diagram 12b*) and leave for about 24 hours to dry and strengthen.

**11** Unstaple and attach with copper tacks or staples to the frame of the screen leaf (*see diagram 12c*).

To finish, the areas of canvas showing between cracks of the leather can be touched in with acrylic paints which will adhere safely to the unprimed canvas. They are also best for retouching as necessary any small losses on the painted surface, as they do not dry out with a brittle film. The edges of the canvas on the leaf frame can be covered with a suitable braiding or leather strip. The leather dressing can now be applied and about four days later a sparse coat of a good white wax polish (see PRODUCTS) and then the whole buffed to a soft sheen.

## Stain removal

Grease marks will generally come away by cautious dabbing with a piece of cotton wool dipped in a few drops of white spirit. Candle wax should have the excess scraped away with a blunt edged instrument, then a piece of white blotting paper should be put over the mark and gentle heat applied with a cool iron so the wax is melted and absorbed.

Usually it is advisable not to try any bleaching because the mark left by the treatment may easily be worse than the one that it removed. Eucalyptus oil on cotton wool will lift quite a few sundry stains of indeterminable origin.

## Upholstery

If this has passed to a state of severe fraying and possibly tearing it is probably best that it should be replaced. If in a sound condition it can be cleaned off with saddle soap, dried and left as it is. Should the colour, however, look washed out, it may be given the most sparing treatment with leather dressing (see *Cleaning*) and then the chair or settee should be kept out of circulation for at least a week.

# Jewellery and Objets d'Art

The precious and the rare that come under this heading will seldom need anything drastic done to them for the sake of restoration. In fact if you think they do call for some specialised attention, take them straight off to the specialist. Nonetheless most of these things that we treasure may never have had even a light clean in their lives, so that beautiful as we may think they look, because we have become accustomed to seeing them like that, really the pinnacle of their beauty is hidden under a veil of grime. Necklaces that grace lovely necks are bound to pick up some make-up; rings set with stones accrue perspiration and dirt; small precious things that are handled can tarnish and become clouded with a skin of refined greasy dust.

Most of these things are picked out from the jewel box, trinket box or special drawer, put on to adorn, or slipped into a pocket or handbag to use and to show for admiration. Later they are put back into their secure little places but never cleaned, almost as though their owners were fearful that these special things might dissolve in water, when in fact a number of them are among the hardest materials around.

When setting out to bring back the sparkle to the family diamonds and the rest, step one is to provide a safe place to work with them. Using the top of a table or desk can be courting loss. If a necklace breaks, or a setting is loose, beads or small stones can roll out of sight through cracks in the wood, and if they land on the floor it may take a fair time to find them, even with a torch held at a raking angle to pick up reflections.

A good, large wooden tray, if possible one of those big ones from a dumb-waiter, can be lined with a piece of old sheet or similar white material, folding it right over the edges and tucking it underneath (*see diagram 13*). Arrange on the table outside the tray the materials and tools that will be needed, including items such as:

*Diagram 13  Equipment set out ready for jewellery cleaning*

Alcohol (pure)
Ammonia
Bowl, 25 cm (10 in) diameter, plastic, with layer of towelling to pad base, for washing and another, for rinsing
Brushes, several artist's small soft-hair
Chamois pieces
Chamois nail buffer
Cotton wool, pulled out into small pieces
Cotton buds
Crocus powder, in pot
Dish containing soapy water
Dish containing detergent and water

Ground rice
Jeweller's eye-glass
Jeweller's rouge, in pot
Methylated spirits
Olive oil
Pincers, small pair
Potato flour, in pot
Powdered magnesia
Silver cleaner, dip type
Toothbrush, soft
Towelling pieces, soft
Tripoli powder, in pot
White spirit
Wood slips, to make tiny swabs

The jeweller's eye-glass is an important item. Use it to examine everything fully for loose stone settings, cracking or other defects. If these are present, don't do it yourself, let the trained one. When using any of the above materials, bring them and containers into the tray. (See *Jewellery* on page 128 for general principles of cleaning.)

## Materials, problems, objects and techniques

### Agate

A semi-precious stone, variegated, often banded chalcedony;

others in the group include cornelian and onyx, which should be treated similarly. Chalcedony was known anciently as Cassidoine. The stones are seldom truly clear, but have a pleasant translucence and a somewhat waxy lustre rather than a real sparkle, so don't go buffing away trying to get one. Agate may be as a pendant, necklace or set in gold or silver as a ring.

As a necklace, it is probably best not to immerse it; rather dip some swabs of cotton wool in soapy water and dab off the dirt. If this has hardened between the stones, loosen with a toothbrush that has been dipped in the soapy water. Try not to get the threading material wetter than necessary. Dry with soft towelling. Next, holding each stone one at a time, give a very light buffing with the nail buffer. Pendants and rings can be gently washed in warm soapy water or detergent. If silver mounted, this can be treated with a proprietary dip type silver cleaner (see PRODUCTS) using a cotton bud and then rinsed.

### Aigrettes
A jewelled clasp most probably made of gold but sometimes of silver, that was originally intended to hold a feather in the cap, hat or hair, but likely to have been used in other ways for some time. The stones can be brushed around with a small paint brush that has been dipped in alcohol, or if this does not shift the dirt, follow up with white spirit. The gold will need little else than a polish with a piece of chamois, and the silver a wiping with a dip type silver cleaner on a cotton bud, then rinse and dry.

### Amber
Never put any spirit solvent anywhere near amber, or else you will start dissolving it. This important warning also applies to toilet waters, perfumes and hair sprays, which may not actively start reducing the size of your earrings or necklace but if they get on to the amber that beautiful sheen will become permanently dulled and the full beauty of this jewellery will be gone for always. If amber does become dirty, all that needs doing is to wash it in warm soapy water, but only do this when really needed. That particular amber gleam can be brought back after washing by applying a little olive oil on a piece of cotton wool and then wiping it off. Amber is a substance that seems to improve with light and its whole being blooms by being in contact with the skin. If unfortunately you do have a break, it may be repaired by using a very thin application of an epoxy adhesive (see PRODUCTS).

Ambroid, which looks like amber, really is amber and not a synthetic, because it is made from chips and small fragments of the real thing that are heated and pressed together. This is used generally for decorative articles, costume jewellery, umbrella handles and the like. Synthetic amber is made from various resins such as copal, also celluloid, camphor and turpentine, all of which may also be given the washing treatment.

## Aquamarine
A somewhat delicate stone that can crack quite easily, particularly in hot water, so always remove rings with these stones in before washing the hands. Lukewarm soapy water is safe for cleaning.

## Cameos
Some of these with deep detail can accumulate unsightly greasy dirt. Tackle this first with a small paint brush which has been dipped in white spirit, gently easing the tip right into the smallest details. Next rinse the brush and dip it into a warm soapy water that has had a few drops of ammonia added. Brush over thoroughly with this and then rinse with the brush dipped in clean warm water. Dry well with a piece of chamois and buff up the mount with the nail buffer. With the treatment, don't overlook the back.

## Censers
Those that date back a couple of hundred years or more are often exquisitely chased and pierced; but they can have considerable staining and deposits from the incense, a resin, and smoke from that and the charcoal. Before attempting to clean the silver of which these are generally made, dip a cotton bud into methylated spirits to which has been added a little ammonia. Work this into the details, both inside and out, and the smoke stains should come away. A cotton bud plus white spirit plus patience will dissolve resin deposits. The whole can then be immersed in a dip type silver cleaner, rinsed in warm soapy water, then in clean water and dried.

## Châtelaines
Originally a clasp or chain worn at the waist by the mistress of the house, various small necessities such as keys being suspended from it.

An antique silver version should first have its appendages

removed and containers emptied, and after that may be cleaned in a dip type cleaner, washed and rinsed and then dried. The small hinges of some of the holders can benefit from a tiny drop of fine oil; put it on with a very small brush, work the lid a few times and afterwards thoroughly wipe off any excess.

## Coral

It is better not to immerse coral in water but to clean off any grime with cotton buds dipped in warm water to which has been added a little detergent; rinse and dry. If there are some deposits that remain obstinate, these can be removed by making a paste of crocus powder or Tripoli powder (see GLOSSARY) with just water; apply gently with a cotton bud and then rinse and dry.

## Diamanté

This should be handled very carefully as the stones are often only stuck into position, so any form of washing can lead to trouble. The safest method of cleaning is a light wipe over with a brush dipped in a little alcohol, then blow on them to evaporate the spirit quickly.

## Diamonds

True diamonds may be washed in warm soapy water, and accretions of greasy grime can be loosened by a brush dipped in methylated spirits and ammonia. Rings that are worn regularly pick up deposits of a surprisingly tenacious nature in behind a clawed setting or circumference setting. It will need patience to worm it all away and you need a very small brush and several applications. Then at last your prize jewel will again really sparkle.

A cautionary point here to be noted: there are those who take advantage of the camouflage of dirty stones. Examples of switches by the unscrupulous are not unheard of. I know of one which involved a splendid platinum bar brooch with a pleasant sized diamond and pearl crossover: an heirloom passed down, and through many hands, and insured for around £600 in the early 1920s. This had been in a nursing-home with its then owner, but when taken by a hopeful legatee recently to sell, the jeweller pointed out that the diamond was now certainly not the original and the pearl was no longer real. Value £16.

Ever since man set out to make diamonds, dealing in such matters has become more and more fraught. True diamonds have actually been made by the General Electric Company in

Schenectady, America. In 1955, from a piece of graphite subjected to an immense pressure and an exceedingly high temperature, a one carat stone emerged – at a cost of many times that of a natural one. But the nasty things you want to watch for if buying second-hand diamonds that are a bit on the grimy side are the diagems, the lithium niobates and even more sophisticated simulants. Regrettably it is not only diamonds the wide fellows are faking: rubies and sapphires and others are on the list; so if offered a bargain covered in dirt, be on your guard.

### Emeralds
Even a little veiling of grease and dirt will take away that lovely deep look of this stone. A little bathing in warm soapy water with a few drops of ammonia will clear, or if some remains, frisk out with a brush dipped in methylated spirits.

### Engraved stones
Depending on their setting, the safest way is to give a first clean back and front with a cotton bud dipped in warm soapy water, and then work into the engraving with a small brush which has been dipped in methylated spirits; be patient, and if necessary, try white spirit as well, but never any of the abrasive powders. Make sure the back is thoroughly cleaned out, as some of these finely engraved stones rely on transmitted light for their full effect.

### Étui
These delightful decorated boxes need differing treatments as there will be various materials present. The box itself may be of fine inlays; these can be handled as suggested in FURNITURE or if it is covered with leather see LEATHER. Inside can be cut-glass scent bottles with silver tops. Rinse out dregs of past perfume with alcohol or methylated spirits; wipe the cut glass with a cloth damped with soapy water and a few drops of ammonia. Treat the silver top with cotton buds dipped in a dip type cleaner. Scissors and small knives should be examined for rust and if present treated as in METALS.

### Ivory
This lovely material needs care in handling. It tends to become more brittle with age and can be affected by excess temperatures that can cause distortion, warping and splitting. It should never be immersed in water or any other liquid for cleaning. In fact any

approach should be with some understanding, for ivory naturally acquires a mellow creamy yellow patina, and also some crafts-men can have introduced decorative staining. Treatment should be little more than a wiping over with some cotton wool or a soft cloth dipped in warm water to which a little gentle detergent has been added; follow this with a swab dipped in clean water and then dry. If it is felt a mild bleaching is really needed, make a stiff paste of whiting with 20 vol. hydrogen peroxide, cover the object evenly and leave on for about an hour; then using cotton wool pieces and a little clear water, rinse away all traces of the paste. When dry a little almond oil can be rubbed over the surface, left for a few minutes and after that wiped off.

Items made by the bachiru technique, in which the craftsman tints the surface of the ivory with colour and then engraves through to expose the underlying natural ivory, should never be touched.

## Jade
It is best wiped over with a soft cloth or piece of cotton wool dip-ped in warm soapy water that has had a few drops of ammonia added to it. A brush may be needed to loosen grime from details, and methylated spirits or white spirit can be used. Some have advocated a light white wax polish on time-abraded areas. This is a matter for personal aesthetics. Possibly a gentle buffing with a soft chamois may give a more satisfactory look.

## Jet
Costume jewellery made with the glittering black Whitby jet came to particular popularity during the reign of Queen Victoria and was worn as a sign of mourning for Prince Albert. To clean, gently rub with soft kneaded new bread. It can be very brittle, so handle with care. Breakages are best attended to with an epoxy, or one of the instant adhesives (see PRODUCTS).

## Jeweller's cement
Also called Armenian cement, it can be made from isinglass, mastic and ammoniac dissolved in alcohol. If a stone in costume jewellery becomes detached the cement should clean off with either alcohol or acetone. Clear traces of the old cement from the setting and reset stone with an epoxy adhesive. If the fit is not very tight you may have to make up a little paste with the epoxy or an instant adhesive with a small amount of kaolin, whiting or marble dust.

## Jeweller's rouge

A red powder, ferric oxide, used for polishing fine metals and other hard surfaces that may have suffered from abrasion. It is gentle and can be used dry or mixed into a paste with water or methylated spirits. Application is best with a piece of chamois, or for small areas a cotton bud. As indicated earlier, take care not to get under fingernails or in quicks, as with some it can cause unpleasant inflammation.

## Jewellery

Before cleaning, in general always examine the setting of the stones with a jeweller's eye-glass (see introduction to this chapter). Those that have a claw or open or circumference setting are normally safe to clean with warm soapy water, then rinse and dry; or they may be cleaned with alcohol, methylated spirits or a proprietary cleaner, except for pearls, opals and turquoise (see separate entries). If the stones are so set that the back is enclosed this will probably indicate that they are glued or set in a cement that could be affected by a liquid, in which case only the slightest surface clean with a damped cotton bud should be attempted. A paste of crocus powder (see GLOSSARY) with methylated spirits might be used with a cotton bud. Be cautious about any buffing up as this could loosen the stones.

## Marcasite

This may be gone over gently with a brush dipped in a paste of crocus or Tripoli powder with methylated spirits. Traces of paste can be removed with a brush dipped in methylated spirits alone. Finish with a delicate buffing with a chamois.

## Netsuke

These miniature Japanese carvings may be made from ivory or wood and were intended to act as a form of button to fix the inrō (or seal-case containing everyday necessities) to the silk cord and belt. As the craftsmen may have used colouring, sfumato (a technique producing a graded, smoky look) and other methods for decoration apart from the carving, these small masterpieces should be given little more than a dusting with a brush and then a gentle buffing up with a chamois. If over-dull, a very sparse application of a good white wax polish could be permissible, followed by a soft cloth or the chamois.

LEFT: Chipped veneer: a corner has been knocked off, exposing the carcass wood; also part of the metal strip inlay is missing. Note how panel pins have regrettably been driven through the upper strip by an earlier owner.

BELOW: Severe blistering and lifting of veneer.

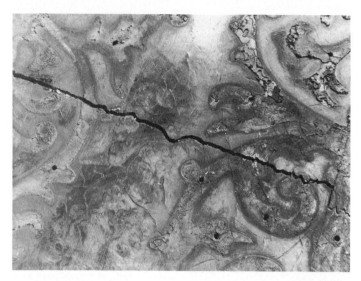

TOP: Veneer splitting after movement of the carcass wood. Heavy brass mounts have been removed for treatment, leaving traces of verdigris.

BOTTOM: Crude removal of an earlier plate and replacement with a more modern version. Badly filled screw holes and little attempt to disguise a botched job.

TOP: A badly broken Dresden ornament of Bacchus and nymphs.

BOTTOM: The same piece in the course of restoration.

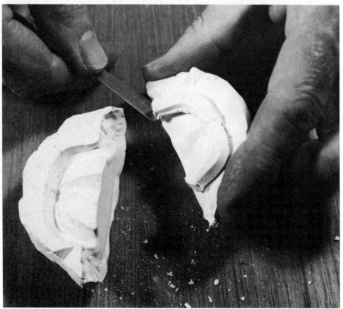

TOP LEFT: One of a pair of late 18th century Derby tureens had a handle missing. A plaster mould is taken from the handle of the good one.

BOTTOM LEFT: Removing the replacement handle from the plaster mould.

ABOVE: The restored tureen lid with its pair. The one at the bottom is the one that was treated.

ABOVE: Repair of broken plate with an epoxy glue; after assembling, strips of strong gummed paper will hold it together while the resin cures.

RIGHT: Repair of ceramics or glass may sometimes call for the insertion of a strengthening dowel. Drilling out needs care and patience.

TOP: Silver cup from Enkomi, Cyprus, as excavated.
BOTTOM: The same cup after restoration.

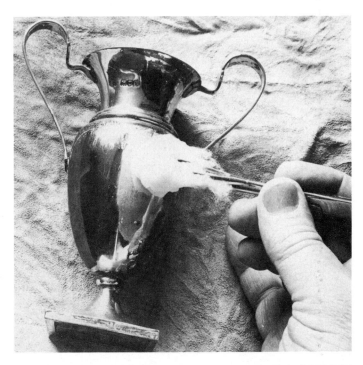

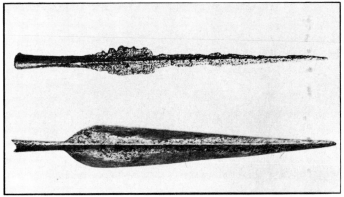

TOP: Cleaning silver with a liquid electrochemical cleaner. Hold the cotton wool swab with forceps or wrap it round a small wooden splint.

BOTTOM: An early Iron Age spearhead, *top* before restoration and *bottom* after treatment with a metal-filled epoxy resin.

ABOVE: An Egyptian cat with a severe attack of bronze disease.

TOP RIGHT: Restoration work on a terracotta bas relief by the 18th century artist Jan van Logteren using an epoxy resin composition.

BOTTOM RIGHT: The effects of climate and pollution on a Japanese carved wooden canopy of the 14th or 15th century. Humidity has caused the wood to split and the copper rings have been badly tarnished by impurities in the atmosphere.

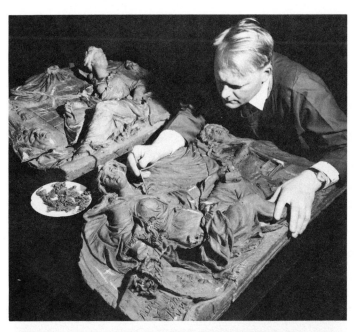

LEFT: A Jacobean chair, circa 1676, from Ham House. Strong light and excessive humidity have caused deterioration and rotting of the silk covering.

BELOW: Warm potato flour being pushed gently down into lace. The flour should be left in position for up to half an hour and then carefully shaken off.

Restoration of a sarcophagus lid at the Fitzwilliam Museum, Cambridge, using an epoxy glue.

Backs of typical 19th century paintings, *top* using a flat bladed knife to remove trapped dirt etc from between canvas and stretcher, *bottom* tightening wedges to remove loose folds from canvas.

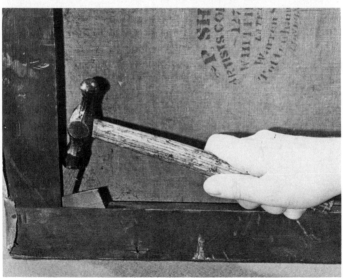

TOP: Damage by sonic boom in the ceiling of the rococo church at Steinhausen, Germany.

BOTTOM: This early 19th century portrait showed excessive asphaltum around the head and eyes, the right side shows the results after cleaning.

Using a cotton bud moistened with the requisite metal dip to clean the metal mount on a mother of pearl faced box.

## Opals
These should not be immersed but treated with cotton buds dipped in warm soapy water, rinsed by a bud dipped in clean water, and dried. They may also be dry cleaned in the same way as *Pearls* below.

## Pearls
These are best cleaned by placing in a tin or small jar with a handful of potato flour (see WHERE TO GET WHAT) or powdered magnesia. Shake the container gently for several minutes and leave the pearls in the powder for at least 24 hours, shake again and leave once more, then a final shake and remove and brush off the powder. Artificial pearls should be cleaned with a damp chamois.

## Perfume bottles
These small objects are usually of glass or ceramics. They should be well rinsed out with methylated spirits to remove any traces of past perfumes; this may take several goes as gummy residual materials with the perfumes can be obstinate. If the tops are of the hinge type, give these a little soaking with the methylated spirits and then a tiny drop of oil. Wipe off excess.

## Pietre dure
Fine and beautiful mosaic, also termed Florentine mosaic, in vogue particularly in Italy during the late Renaissance. It was made with tesserae cut from semi-precious stones which could include cornelian, jasper, lapis lazuli, onyx and porphyry, and also selected fine marbles, and sometimes even diamonds, gold and silver; ivory was put in low relief. If the fortunate possessor of a tablet of pietre dure, I would do little more to it, having examined it for any looseness, than caress-polish it with a piece of fine chamois. With such a possession if any defects show up, it is wise to consult a specialist.

## Rock crystal
Craftsmen have worked this hard member of the quartz family for centuries, creating jewellery, drinking cups and small exquisite objects from it. Often it will be set in precious metals or mounted with them and also many combinations of the decorative arts: chasing, engraving, repoussé, enamelling, and set with semi-precious and precious stones. Give a thorough examination to see that all parts are firm. Then the object may be cleaned by

using swabs of cotton wool or cotton buds dipped in warm soapy water to which a few drops of ammonia have been added. Use a brush to get at fine details, if necessary dipped in methylated spirits or white spirit. Rinse with swabs and clean water and dry. The gold mounts can be gently buffed with chamois and the silver where present may be treated with dip, which should then be rinsed off and the mounts dried.

There is a pleasant little legend about rock crystal dating from medieval times: it was said to be a protection against poison, for if it was brought near to poison it would promptly discolour and warn whoever it was who was threatened.

### Rubies

Although rating close to the diamond for hardness, the ruby can be prone to chip and so should be treated with care when cleaning. Use a cotton bud or small brush with warm soapy water; rinse and dry. To finish, gently rub the surface with a piece of chamois dipped in alcohol.

### Sapphires

Like rubies, very hard, but they can be prone to damage from heat; even hand-hot water has been known to crack them. Cleanse with a cotton bud and warm soapy water, rinse and dry. Surfaces may be gently wiped in the same way as a ruby with a chamois and alcohol.

### Snuff boxes

These little things are often demonstrations of a craftsman's skill in using precious metals, with engraving, repoussé work, chasing, enamelling or work with inlaid precious or semi-precious stones. They have also been made of wood, lesser metals, bone, ivory, horn and tortoiseshell. If the lids have a hinge this can be given a tiny drop of oil, work it to and fro and wipe off excess. Gold can be buffed up with a chamois, silver can be treated with a dip. Bone may be gently bleached with a 2% solution of Chloramine T, obtainable from a chemist, and rinsed. For the rest, a sparse application of a good white wax polish (see PRODUCTS) and a finishing with a soft cloth or pieces of cotton wool.

### Tassies

Simulants of precious stones made by James Tassie (1735–99) who worked with a physician, Henry Quin, and developed a type of vitreous paste that could take on the look and some of the characteristics of particularly antique gems. They could still be around, for one cataloguer of his production estimated that some 15,800 were made. Again, as with other precious stone simulants, if they are dirty and in grubby settings they can fool. The phoney jewel people will try anything: a slip of polished metal foil under a cut-glass 'stone', washes of colour to deck out chunks of glass as bargain rubies or sapphires. In this trade, resist all bargains you know nothing about. As many of the simulants may be set in some kind of cement or glue, they should be cleaned with care, either with a cotton bud dipped in methylated spirits or just a soft rub with a chamois. A light application of a paste of water or methylated spirits mixed with crocus powder might be used and then remnants of the paste removed with a brush.

## Tortoiseshell

The best will have come from the hawksbill and may be found used for inlays and made into fan frames, card-cases, snuff boxes and ornamental combs. It may also have silver and gold let into it and have mounts, particularly of silver. This metal can be treated with a cotton bud and dip but with all care that the dip does not get on to the tortoiseshell. The shell itself can be washed with warm soapy water, rinsed and dried. The surface may be given a treatment with a good white wax polish (see PRODUCTS) or wiped over with a drop or two of almond oil. If the surface has become unpleasantly abraded, this is possible to remedy by rubbing on a paste of crocus powder (see GLOSSARY) or jeweller's rouge mixed with methylated spirits. It is best applied with a piece of chamois. Breaks can be repaired with an epoxy put on very thin, or with an instant glue.

## Turquoise

The stones should not be immersed in water but may be cleaned with a cotton bud dipped in methylated spirits. They can also be given a dry cleaning as suggested with pearls.

# Paintings

Painters working on wooden panels and canvas or other textiles on wooden stretchers have used a variety of media for expression, diverse not only in materials but also in their reaction to conditions around them. Before treatment it is necessary to identify the method in which the painter worked. Basically the colours which an artist uses are the same whichever medium he employs. The differences with the methods are the vehicles – oils, varnishes and other liquid or paste substances – that are mixed with the colours. Although some pigments may be acted on by light and other sources, it is principally the vehicle which in time can cause trouble.

Paintings on canvas or wooden panels are complicated sandwiches of a variety of materials which should be permanent if the artist has prepared his support properly, but if some steps have been skimped or if the paintings are subjected to excessive damp or heat, severe damage can be caused.

A painting on a wooden panel starts with the wood itself and on to this the painter would first lay *gesso grosso*, a mixture of basically a whiting and a glue (which was very often made from rabbit-skin), or he might use the casein curds from soured milk. The gesso is prepared in a double boiler and poured or brushed on to the support in thicknesses of upwards of one eighth of an inch. When this has dried he lays on the top *gesso sottile*, a much more liquid and finer form of gesso. Then, if he was working as some of the early German or Flemish painters did using gold leaf, he would put on a thin coat of bole, a fine reddish earth, and on top of this, when dry, glair, a mixture of beaten egg white and water. On to the glair while still tacky, the gold leaf was laid, and finally his paint layers and varnish.

With a painting on canvas, first of all the canvas is sized to prevent any oil from rotting the material; next over the size goes a priming which may be one or other of several substances: in the past it was often lead white; today it is more likely to be a white

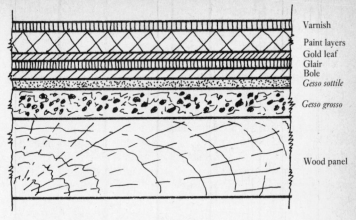

Varnish

Paint layers
Gold leaf
Glair
Bole
*Gesso sottile*

*Gesso grosso*

Wood panel

*Diagram 14 Section through an oil painting on a wooden panel*

emulsion. After this many painters like to lay an *imprimatura,* an overall veiling of colour to kill the white of the priming. Then the paint layers are applied, which may be in the form of under-painting and afterwards the heavy over-painting, and lastly the varnish.

A painting on canvas is more prone to damage by mishandling because it can be dented very easily; also there is the fact that high humidity can easily attack the canvas at the back and cause the size to swell which can lift the priming and paint layers. Paintings on wood panels are not so liable to damage by handling but they will be prone to attack from woodworm which have been known to eat their way not only through the timber but through the layers of gesso and paint right through to the surface. They are also liable to damage from damp which can cause mould growths.

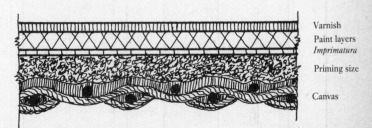

Varnish
Paint layers
*Imprimatura*

Priming size

Canvas

*Diagram 15 Section through an oil painting on canvas*

Below is a list of the main methods artists have used, to assist in identifying how your picture was painted, drawn or printed.

## Principal techniques

### Acrylic

Introduced about twenty years ago, the pigments are ground with polymerised synthetic resins. The vehicle being an emulsion responds in many ways similar to tempera, the paint film drying out to a matt, waterproof surface. As the acrylic vehicle is in itself a strong adhesive, this method of painting has given the artist considerable freedom, and acrylic pictures can be painted on a wide variety of supports including canvas, hessian, sailcloth, other textiles, paper, card, panels, hardboard, metal sheets, ceramic plaques and glass.

The paint film, once dry, retains a certain elasticity and is little affected by heat, cold or damp, and even atmospheric pollutants will do minimal damage.

The pictures can generally be recognised by the fact that the colours tend not to achieve the full rich translucence and power of oils and there will be little evidence of any overall craquelure. If cracking or flaking does appear on an acrylic painting, it is likely that the painter will have mixed oils or oil painting media with his colours.

### Alkyd

Introduced in 1976, these colours represent a new medium in their own right and an extension of the oil painting manner. The name Alkyd is derived from the word 'Alcid' which was coined by the scientist Kienle in 1927 to indicate a substance made from alcohols and acids. As the colours can be worked in a like manner to oils, the varnished film appears similar but perhaps not quite so rich in pigment power.

### Casein

A milk protein that can be used as a vehicle for pigments, the resulting paint film having a matt sheen similar to tempera. Initially soluble in water, once dry the surface is water resistant but very brittle; thus casein colours should only be used on a firm, movement-free support, for if the colours are too thick there is a likelihood of cracking.

Although curd glue was used by the early Egyptians, the Greeks, the Romans and the Hebrews, and is mentioned as an adhesive in 11th-century manuscripts, it does not appear to have been used as a vehicle for pigments until the 18th century. Atmospheric pollutants, particularly ammonia, can affect the film, and the pictures are best kept behind glass.

## Distemper

Occasionally artists used low grade colours which have as their vehicle a simple water-soluble glue that will probably not have great adhesion. Pictures can generally be recognised by a rather coarse-grained matt surface and the fact that deep, rich colours will be absent. They are best kept behind glass and not exposed to high relative humidity.

## Encaustic

One of the oldest methods of painting, and the one favoured by the early Egyptians with their so-called mummy paintings from the tombs. It is almost obsolete today.

It was evolved by the ancient Greeks, and takes its name from the Greek *enkaustikos* meaning literally 'burning in'. It involves the application of colours with hot wax to a support that may be plaster, stone, wood or card, and it can be manipulated by the use of heated spatulas. Damage can be caused by moisture seeping through from the back of the support, and the front is susceptible to abrasion. Exposure to excess heat and cold should be avoided.

## Oils

This technique was gradually evolved during the 13th, 14th and 15th centuries, as artists sought greater richness and power with their painting. Although its invention has always been credited to the Van Eyck brothers, this is not correct. Exploratory steps in adding oil and varnish to egg tempera to increase richness were taken by some early Italians, and later Antonello da Messina (1430–1479) was a notable experimenter. Probably most oil paintings have been carried out on canvas on wooden stretchers, and for all the media used by artists, more trouble has been met with oils than with any other; the reason being that not only, as mentioned earlier, may the steps of preparing the support have been skimped, but also artists such as Sir Joshua Reynolds experimented with so-called 'fugitive' pigments such as bitumen, which can do quite terrible things to a picture, bleeding into other colours, and when varnished, drying out to leave an 'alligator-skin-like' surface. After about fifty years all paintings start developing a characteristic fine cracking right over the surface of the paint; this is less noticeable on a wooden panel, more so on a canvas. It is caused largely, certainly with canvas, by the movement of the support, the action of moisture, heat and cold, and is to be expected in paintings prior to 1850. In fact if you are buying an oil of the early part of the 18th century and the paint film presents a perfect smooth and uncracked surface, be very suspicious: either an over-zealous restorer will have over-painted considerably, or it is a fake.

## Tempera

This is a somewhat misleading term that is often loosely applied to methods where the pigments are mixed with a variety of strange substances, not only water-soluble glues but also plant juices such as fig-milk and egg white, or the whole egg. True tempera, as used by many of the earlier painters and by artists of today, is when the pigments are mixed with egg yolk alone – plus a little water to give fluidity if needed – and sometimes a little preservative. The egg needs to be very fresh, and after the yolk has been separated from the white, the sac is carefully held up between thumb and forefinger over a saucer and stabbed with a clean blade so that the pure yolk can escape and the membrane of the sac be discarded.

Of all painting media tempera is the most permanent because there is little physically that can go wrong with the film. It is highly unlikely that it will crack, and once dry it is remarkably resistant to dirt and surface cleaning. It was greatly in favour in the early 14th and 15th centuries and many of the exquisite jewel-like pictures of the early Flemish artists which appear at first to be oil, are actually egg tempera that has been varnished. The ideal support for tempera is the gesso panel; the paint surface is matt with a subtle sheen. Although early painters did varnish their pictures, it is unwise to varnish a tempera painting without understanding the tonal changes that can take place since varnishing can considerably alter the tone value of a number of pigments, notably blues and brown earths.

Paintings by their very nature are probably more prone to damage than other works of art. Therefore, when a picture is of any rarity or value, it is wise to ask advice from a trained restorer; but there are a number of treatments that can safely be given in the home if proper care is taken. Pictures should ideally be inspected at least twice a year, and not only the surface but also the canvas, stretchers, hanging attachments to the frames, and cords and wires, be examined.

## Materials, problems, products and processes

### Backs of paintings on canvas
It is always worth protecting the back of a canvas from physical damage and this is quite simply done, depending on size, by using a sheet of stiff cardboard or hardboard and attaching it with screws to the frame (not to the wooden stretcher). Drill a few holes along the top and bottom to allow for ventilation.

### Blisters and flaking
These conditions are generally brought on by the actions of moisture causing the size on the canvas to swell, thus pushing up the layers of the priming and paint. It may also be caused, particularly with flaking, by acute low humidity where the atmosphere has become so dry that the binding materials lose adhesion and become desiccated, and in bad cases the top layers of paint can fall away. Blistering and flaking are very much in the province of the trained restorer, who will know how to re-attach the loosened paint, generally with a substance such as a wax resin mixture and an electric spatula. The blistering and flaking should be caught as early as possible, and it can help when examining a picture to use a raking light that will show up the little disturbances in the paint film.

### Bloom
This condition – which resembles very much the kind of misty look on some black grape skins – can appear over an oil painting, generally on darker earth colours. The condition is probably brought on by excessive damp combined with chilling of the atmosphere. Fortunately, it is often quite easily removed by gently wiping the surface of the painting with a piece of soft cotton rag or cotton wool. If it is more obstinate, it can be treated with a high quality picture wax-varnish. The condition usually occurs with old paintings that still have their original varnish or which have been re-varnished with one of the natural resin varnishes such as copal, damar or mastic. Today's synthetic picture varnishes are not only frequently water clear but also very

unlikely to bloom, and more than this, it is probable they will have had a plasticiser added to prevent cracking.

## Buttoning

This is a term for treating thin wood panels which are cracking or have split. First, spread a sheet of soft cotton material over the working support, which should be firm and flat, then lay the panel face down on this, the surface of the paint being first protected by a sheet of plastic film. Cut small squares, about 25 mm (1 in) in measurement, from quality hardwood, with a thickness not more than about 6–9 mm (¼–³⁄₈ in). These pieces should be sanded to fit exactly to the chosen sites on the splits or cracks,

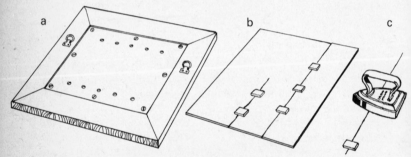

*Diagram 16 a  Hanging rings and backing in place with ventilation holes*
   *b  Wood battens on cracks and splits*
   *c  Apply weight while adhesive sets*

and spaced out about three to four inches apart. If the splits are opening slightly, the panel will have to be held tightly in position with special clamps. Glues may be Scotch or other water types or one of the synthetics suitable for wood. Be very careful that the glue, particularly the synthetic type, does not get through on to the paint surface. After placing the buttons in position, put a weight on them and leave for 48 hours.

## Canvas and stretchers

Even top quality canvas will need some treatment after fifty years or more, as, depending upon the environment and the way it was originally prepared by the artist, the fibres can weaken and there is a danger that it will tear away from the stretchers. What is needed is re-lining. Re-lining is the application of a new canvas behind the old which is fixed with an adhesive such as beeswax and damar resin. This is very much the premise of the professional, and it should *never* be attempted in the home.

It is important to inspect the canvas and the stretchers as a whole, particularly where the tacks have been put in. Some of the early iron tacks are very prone to rust which will cause rotting in these areas. It may be possible, if the canvas is sound apart from this, to fix it more firmly in position by driving in copper tacks between the iron ones, if possible removing the remains of the iron tacks. To do this, rest the canvas vertically on a firm basis and use a light hammer.

The stretchers themselves will generally have mitred corners with small wedges and if ripples or folds are developing in the canvas, by careful tapping of these wedges into the joints, a gentle stretching can be given. Once again, stand the canvas on a firm surface, and work your way round the corners using a small hammer.

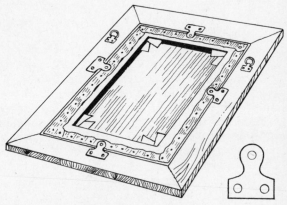

*Diagram 17 Shelf ears securing canvas in place*

Sometimes accretions of dust and dirt and odd objects – such as holly berries from Christmas decorations or fragments of plaster from the ceiling – can fall down and become trapped between the back of the canvas and the stretcher, causing small bumps to appear on the surface of the painting. If these are neglected, the paint can easily crack and may flake away. Take the picture out of the frame and lay it face down on a soft cloth on a firm table and then, using a trowel-shaped painting knife with a cranked handle or a plastic spatula, very cautiously feel your way along between the canvas and the stretcher, carefully dragging out the offending materials. The results can be sometimes quite surprising. My best find, on a very large double portrait, was some ancient butler's fountain pen.

## Cleaning

Paintings which are hung unglazed inevitably pick up mess from the atmosphere – one offender being nicotine – and also a surprising amount of grease and sticky dirt can be in the air, particularly in industrial and urban areas. This can normally be removed quite safely by using a proprietary picture cleaner (see PRODUCTS). It is important to follow meticulously the instructions with the bottle and only work over a small area at a time, having one piece of cotton wool for the cleaner and another for white spirit or turpentine substitute, to remove the cleaner after the job is done. It is not safe to use any cleaner with a spirit base on pictures which are less than about thirty years old. In any case, when using it, keep looking at the swab of cotton wool with the cleaner on to make sure that no colour or flakes of paint are coming off. These proprietary picture cleaners will take off certainly deposits of nicotine and much of the grime on the surface of a painting, but they will not take off old varnishes.

In the past, the only varnishes available were natural resin ones, all of which darken, particularly copal; and thus many pictures have acquired that 'old master' look. Strangely enough, in the middle of the last century this was in fashion, and it is said that some dealers even had the audacity to smother paintings by Constable with this dark treacly substance – his beautiful fresh landscape look not then being the 'in thing'. The removal of these old hardened varnishes is strictly the province of the trained restorer, since all kinds of troubles may arise, and the unwary hand could very speedily damage a fine painting.

A badly cracked surface is dangerous to clean and should be left until professional advice can be sought. Unvarnished paintings can cause trouble and, again, if of quality, should be left to the professional.

## Cradling

This implies a treatment for a badly cracked and rather thick wooden panel and one that may even be in two or three pieces. On the back the conservator fits a system of cross battening so designed that it will allow for some movement of the panel once repaired.

## Fly spots

These unsightly blemishes can cause trouble as they can adhere very strongly to the paint surface. Be very careful to resist the temptation of scraping with a finger nail or some instrument, as it

is quite easy to abrade or damage the paint surface. A very valuable painting should be left to the expert. If not so valuable, an
attempt to remove fly spots can be first made with a cotton bud
slightly moistened with water. Should this not be successful, try
another cotton bud with white spirit; use a little patience and
keep the amount of liquid to the absolute minimum.

## Folk remedies
All too often one hears of the value of cut onions and potatoes to
clean oil paintings and other pictures on canvas or wooden
panels. Please *no*, because – although onions particularly are
cleaning agents – they leave behind a legacy for possible damage
in the future. The juices can penetrate through cracks in the
paint surface and cause trouble with the priming and especially
the sizing of the canvas.

## Framing and glazing
The types of mouldings available for canvas and wood panel
paintings vary considerably. The most important point is that the
one chosen should have sufficient strength in itself to support the
picture satisfactorily. Personal taste enters into this to a high
degree, but try to select a moulding and treatment of the whole
frame that will complement your picture without overpowering
it. In the 19th century there was a vogue for huge, over-wide,
heavily decorated and gilded frames which often completely
smothered the fine paintings they carried. Not only wood was
used but some very large frames were even cast in a form of con-
crete, the weight being almost sufficient to crack the sturdiest
wall. In earlier centuries, 16th and 17th, the fashion was for quite
simple mouldings, commonly with a dark finish.

The canvas or panel should not be nailed into the frame so
that it is immovable; immovability can cause trouble where there
is central heating, as one wood may work against another, and
also the action of heavily hammering a nail into position can
cause cracking to a picture and to the frame itself. Small brass
plates called 'shelf ears' can be bought from an ironmonger, and
four or more of these can be screwed on to the frame only, leaving the part of the shelf ear over the picture unfixed.

When oil paintings are hung on a wall, it often helps if they are
given a slight cant forwards which can stop ugly reflected lights.
It will also prevent a lot of dust from falling on to the surface of
the picture. This is simple to achieve by putting the screw eye or
hanging plate about a third of the way down from the top. Always

make sure that the hanging cords, wires or chains are adequate for the weight of the picture which is being hung.

Glazing of oil paintings, acrylics and pictures in general, on canvas and wood panels, is to a degree a matter of taste, or it may be essential with some delicate surfaces. The main trouble is that you get ugly reflected lights from the glass, which make the picture difficult to appreciate. There is now available non-reflective glass and this, with certain pictures, is certainly well worth the extra expense. When fitting glass in a frame for a picture, make sure there is a narrow fillet about 3 mm (⅛ in) thick between the glass and the picture itself so that the paint surface does not actually touch the glass.

### Holes
An elderly canvas is a delicate substance and can very easily be torn or holed; for instance, a careless handling of a nearby ornament and the damage is done. As far as possible this needs to be treated quickly by an expert, but you may have to give first aid. Take the picture from the frame, and lay it face down on a level surface with a protective film of plastic sheeting. Then repair with tape about an inch wide which has a non-water soluble adhesive, to prevent the edges curling up and causing possible paint losses.

### Household polishes
*Never under any circumstances be tempted to use household polishes on the surface of a picture.* Most polishes are perfectly safe for furniture and other objects, but it is possible that some of the constituents could attack the paint surface. In fact, it is not unknown for an over-zealous cleaner to attempt to brighten up a gilt frame with one or other of the aerosol polishes. It might brighten a gilt frame, but it can cause much damage to the paint film of the picture.

### Moulds
Again, inspect at least twice a year for signs of mould or fungus growths, not only on the surface of the picture but also on the back. If these are present, it generally means that the place the picture is hanging in is over-damp and there is stagnant air from lack of ventilation. Treatment can be to move the picture and generally, once it has dried out, the offending substances can be lightly brushed off with a soft-hair brush. If persistent, consult an expert.

## Picture lights

These can very much add to the enjoyment of paintings in certain dark rooms. Take care, however, that the wiring and parts of the fitting at the back are not in a position to damage the canvas.

## Security devices

Some collectors with very fine paintings quite rightly use tremblers or other warning devices (see SECURITY). These should never be stuck actually on to the canvas, as it has been found that some of the synthetic glues needed to fix the plastic or metal object in place may penetrate and cause considerable disruption to the paint surface. Fix the device to the stretcher, the stretcher bars, or the frame.

## Varnishing

Although the natural resin varnishes such as damar, copal and mastic can still be bought, it is far better to choose one of the clear synthetic varnishes, which not only will not bloom but which will also be unlikely to crack, as these varnishes generally have a plasticising agent with them, and furthermore they will not darken with time. Never apply a varnish to an oil painting that is less than twelve months old. Use a flat white hog-hair varnish brush about 50 mm (2 in) wide, try to choose a dry, warm day, and select a place with good light so that you can observe your progress. Apply the varnish sparingly with small cross strokes, and watch that there are no varnish runs which will be unsightly once dried out. Synthetic varnishes normally will dry in two to three hours. Varnishes may also be bought in aerosol cans and these will need careful application to make sure that the coat is of even thickness. Varnishing can be carried out with the picture flat on a table or vertically on an easel, it's a matter of taste and practice.

It should be pointed out that with some paint films, tempera and acrylic in particular, varnishing can cause quite considerable tonal changes.

## Waxing

This can be used as an alternative surface protection to varnish. For some, the glitter of a fresh varnish film may be discordant, and it is feasible to use a special picture wax polish (see PRODUCTS) that can be purchased from an art dealer. This should have a high percentage of beeswax or synthetic waxes, and it may be applied to the surface of the picture either with a soft rag or piece of cotton wool; or if there is heavy impasto with large areas of ridged paint, it is best put on with a round hog-bristle brush. Polishing can be done with cotton wool, a soft cloth or a soft brush. The resulting surface will be a sheen somewhat comparable to that of an eggshell. Be careful that the wax paste is put on evenly and that no lumps are left caught up in the impasto.

## Woodworm

As with any antique objects or even the house itself, inspection should be made at least twice a year to be certain these pests have not started an invasion. If woodworm is in the frame, after removing the picture it is safe to treat the frame yourself, watching, of course, that the gilding or surface front treatment of the frame is not affected. If the woodworm has got into the stretchers or the wooden panel, it may be wise to consult an expert, because some of the constituents of the liquids for killing woodworm can attack the paint films. A word of warning, if you are having your whole house treated, be careful that the operatives fully understand about pictures, because I have come across a case where a very lovely portrait by Alan Ramsay which was in a badly woodwormed frame was liberally overkilled for woodworm by a commercial operative, with the result that the paint film was quite severely damaged and this was a costly business for the owner.

Woodworm, mould and fungus can all be discouraged by the use of a substance such as formaldehyde, which can be put in solution and lightly sprayed over the back of the picture and the frame. Even more effective can be a saturated solution of thymol in alcohol; apply by a fine spray over the back and this will give protection for quite an appreciable period.

One last word for the over-enthusiastic spring cleaner. One lady I knew, come the season of the year, literally washed her house from top to bottom. This included not only all the curtains – quite all right – but also fine antique furniture – a rather dubious process – and some quite good oil paintings – a very bad idea. As mentioned earlier, moisture can penetrate through the surface of a cracked paint film and cause the size on the canvas to swell, thus bringing on blistering and flaking, and also residual traces of the soap or detergent used could encourage mould growths and more trouble. So please never, *never*, try to clean a painting with water, soap or detergent.

# Drawings and prints

Although it is thought that the art of making paper started in China around AD 105, paper for general use did not appear in Europe until the 12th century. It is likely that the invention was brought from the Far East by the Turks during the Dark Ages. For the artist, paper can be divided into two categories, cartridge and rag. The first of these is made from wood pulp and is generally used for schools or draughtsman's work, whilst rag papers are produced from good quality cotton or linen rags and finished to three surfaces: 'Hot Pressed' with a smooth, slightly shiny finish; 'Not' which is matt; and 'Rough', a paper which in some cases can be coarse-grained and very heavy. Variations of these types have been introduced by individual makers and craftsmen for specialised work and print making. All works on paper are delicate; they require very careful handling and should always be kept either mounted in a frame or in a folio. They can be susceptible to light and should not be hung where the sun's rays can fall directly upon them. A great many techniques have been used by artists both for drawing and print making; the principal methods are listed below.

## Drawing methods

### Chalk
Usually white or very pale colours to heighten or give accents to other forms of drawing.

### Charcoal
One of the oldest of the media for drawing. Depending on the type of charcoal used, it can produce a beautiful range of silvery greys right through to a dense black if a vine charcoal is employed.

## Crayons
These are sticks where the pigments are bound with wax and some hardening additive such as shellac and include the ordinary wax crayon, Conte, bistre and sanguine.

## Gouache
Closely allied to water colour, the technique implies the use of body or opaque colours. The paint film will be matt and may with some artists have traces of impasto.

## Mixed media
This implies that the artist has combined several methods together; ink and water colour, crayon and wash, pastel and gouache, or sometimes three or four media. Works carried out in this manner are very delicate and should be treated with the greatest respect and care.

## Pastel
Here the pigments are prepared – usually with an inert substance to bulk them or mix them to the right shade – and bound together under pressure with perhaps a minimum of gum tragacanth or sometimes the curd from soured milk. Pastel drawings are very fragile and should never be knocked, as the colour can fall away from the paper.

## Pen and ink
Many of the early artists used quills taken from swans and geese. Oriental draughtsmen employed large grasses and thin bamboos. Steel nibs of various shapes started to appear late in the 18th century. Other substances used for making nibs include horn and tortoiseshell. Inks may range from black to bistre, sepia and almost all the colours available. Some artists have worked on moistened paper which gives an attractive 'bleeding' look sometimes confused with water colour.

## Pencil
Lumps of graphite or pencils as we know them today can range in hardness from 9H through to 7B.

## Silverpoint
A method of drawing in which the artist uses a stylus with a silver point. The paper is specially prepared with a wash of calcined bone which leaves a gentle abrasive texture. It is difficult to see

where the lines are, as only minute traces of silver are left on the calcined bone surface. After several days' exposure to the air, these traces tarnish producing the characteristic subtle colour of the silverpoint line.

### Water colour
Pigments which are often transparent bound with some water soluble gum, a little glycerine may be added.

---

# Print making methods

These are divided into three categories, relief, intaglio and flatbed. In the relief print the artist removes areas from the block that he wishes to leave as white, in intaglio prints the artist removes areas from the plate which he wishes to have as black. Flatbed is where the print is made from a plate or stone – as for lithography – or by a form of stencil as with silk screen. Relief methods include lino-cut, woodcut, wood engraving, chiaroscuro woodcut.

### Intaglio
The intaglio techniques are principally concerned with etching and engraving. Etching is where the artist works on a highly polished plate of copper or zinc which has first been given a ground of wax, asphaltum, shellac and other substances; he draws into it with a needle, applying his tonal areas by shading, and then the back of the plate is covered with an acid-resistant varnish and the whole put into a bath of acid so that the design can be eaten out. It is a process that has to be watched very carefully because if the line is made too deep it can eat underneath where the ground still stands and cause a breakaway of the line when printing. To make the print, the ink is rubbed into the plate so that the lines are full and then the standing surface is wiped almost clean with various textiles, the aim being to leave just a faint veil of ink. There is also a technique known as soft ground etching. In this the artist places a piece of thin strong paper over a softer ground on the plate and works with a pencil; when the paper is pulled away the ground adheres to the paper where the pencil lines have been made. Aquatint is another form. A speckled ground is put on the plate and then the artist works with a brush, laying various areas of acid-resistant varnish and

building up to an effect somewhat similar to a brush drawing. Close to this is sugar aquatint where the design is brushed on to the plate with a mixture of a carbon black, sugar and some form of glue; when dry, stopping-out varnish, which is acid-resistant, is painted over, and then the plate is left for several hours in water. In some magic way the water penetrates where the brush drawing is, the sugar mixture swells and lifts the varnish away.

Metal engraving has been carried out on copper, zinc and steel plates using a burin or graver. Mezzotint is a somewhat sophisticated method of engraving that was first invented in 1642 by Ludwig von Siegen. With this technique the plate is first roughened by an instrument called a 'rocker' that covers the whole surface with tiny little pricks, and then highlights and the various tones are worked into it with scrapers and burnishers.

One characteristic of all intaglio prints is that they are printed under high pressure; thus just outside the printed area you get a plate mark. This should be guarded almost as carefully as the print itself because if it is cut off, the value of the print will drop dramatically.

### Flatbed

Flatbed printing first became used with the invention of lithography which works on the principle of the mutual repulsion of grease and water. The drawing is made either with a wax crayon or wax ink on a stone or plate and the print is taken by the stone or plate being damped with water. It was developed by Aloysius Senefelder in 1798. Serigraphy or silk-screen printing is a development principally of the 20th century and does allow for a fairly simple method of printing in numerous colours. There is one other method which is known as monotype. With this the artist paints his design with very thick colours directly on to a sheet of glass, a sheet of metal or a hard surface similar to formica, and to take the print presses a piece of paper directly into the moist colour. It is a very free printing method but only one print can be taken of each design.

## Materials, problems and processes

### Candle wax

Prints in particular seem very prone to collect these marks. One way is to put a piece of clean blotting paper each side of the spot and apply gentle heat from a domestic iron at its lowest setting. The process can be repeated but each time use clean blotting paper. If some traces still remain, they can generally be taken out with white spirit.

## Coffee and tea stains

Damp the area around the stain with cold water then, using a clean brush or a cotton bud, dab on a 2% solution of potassium perborate. Leave the print to dry for two or three hours in sunlight to bleach out the stain.

## Dirt on prints

Provided the ink is stable and the paper not perished, a certain amount of surface cleaning can be carefully carried out with the groom stick mentioned in the list of cleaning materials.

## Fixing

Many of the drawings carried out with sensitive materials such as chalk, charcoal, pastel, soft pencil, may need fixing to stabilise them. However, expert advice should first be sought, since fixative liquids can often seriously affect the tonal values, particularly of pastel. If the drawing is not of great value, it may be fixed by using one or other of the proprietary liquids on the market. These come in aerosols or bottles that can be sprayed with a mouth atomiser. The spray should be directed from a position about a foot away from the drawing, and applied with a number of light coats. Be careful not to put too much on or you will flood the drawing and cause it to bleed seriously.

## Foxing

One of the most prevalent troubles with works on paper is 'foxing'. This appears as small orange brown spots which can quickly grow to perhaps even half an inch or more across. The colour can also be brown or a purple which is almost black. The cause is over-dampness, which results in the size present in most older papers deteriorating and decomposing, leaving a breeding ground for fungus spores which cause the staining. Small areas can be treated by a mixture of equal parts of industrial methylated spirits and hydrogen peroxide. Spot this on with either a soft brush or a cotton bud, then rinse gently with distilled water. If the print has serious overall foxing, it will probably have to be immersed in a large dish and one of the best bleaches to use with this approach is Chloramine T (2% solution), which is mild and will leave nothing of a corrosive nature in the paper. Watch the bleaching very carefully and when you feel it is complete, remove the print and put into another dish with just distilled water. Swirl it around, then remove, mop off excess water with sheets of white blotting paper, and spread out to dry on a flat surface such as a sheet of glass.

## Framing and mounting

The choice of frames is very much an individual decision; the main point is that the moulding should have sufficient strength in itself to support the size of the picture. The mount should be of good quality card and the window cut with precision. This can be quite a tricky business and it is often best to get a professional to do the job. Fixing the drawing or print to the mount should be done using what are called 'guards', small strips of paper, and a good quality paste should be used. If the paper of the drawing or print is very thin it may be very slightly damped and then stuck into position so that when it dries it will become taut and flat. As far as possible avoid hanging water colours, gouaches or pastels in direct sunlight.

## Insect attack

There are two little pests that may be encountered, the first is silverfish. This likes to live on moulds and old decaying glues and pastes in damp surroundings. It will also attack some kinds of paper. The other nuisance can be the firebrat. This is a strange little fellow, rather hairy and whiskery, somewhat like a tiny lobster. It will also eat old glues and pastes but unlike the silverfish likes very dry surroundings. Both of these pests can be discouraged by spraying the back of the mount and the drawing lightly with either formaldehyde or a saturated solution of thymol in alcohol.

## Oil and grease stains

These may be removed with pyridine which can be obtained from a chemist, and this should be applied with a small soft brush or cotton bud. Do the work where there is adequate ventilation.

## Pastels, chalk and charcoal drawings

All three of these, and particularly pastel, can be very delicate and if the picture is of any worth at all, always consult a professional. Tonal changes can take place with treatment and with some old pastels it is very easy to remove almost all the colour. The colours may not be fixed and may be just holding precariously to the light tooth of the paper.

## Removal of varnish

Sadly, in the late 19th century and the early years of this century, there was a fashion for coating prints with ugly, disfiguring, thick yellow copal varnish. With care, it is possible to remove this. It is best, however, to make some experiments with various solvents on the edge of the varnished print. The first attempt could be a mixture of methylated spirits and turpentine substitute which can be gradually strengthened by increasing the quantity of methylated spirits, or a solvent such as acetone. If this latter is used, very good ventilation should be available. A non-spirit solvent can be a 5% solution of ammonia in distilled water. Once a reasonably safe solvent has been worked out, place the print on a sheet of glass and lower into a dish containing the solvent. If the varnish has been unevenly applied, the solvent can be gently stirred with a feather or a soft paintbrush during the operation. It should be pointed out that cleaning a print, particularly an old one, can be a risky business. Some of the artists concocted strange recipes for inks which can become fugitive when immersed in even quite weak solvents.

A number of prints have been hand-painted with water colours and then again subjected to this vandalism of varnish. With care, these can also be treated with similar solvents to those mentioned above, but on no account disturb the action of the solvent with a brush if there is water colour present as this may bring the colour away. After any treatment, leave to dry flat on the sheet of glass.

## Washing

An overall grimy print may be cleansed by immersion in distilled water with a little good quality soap or a wetting agent such as 'Lissapol' or 'Nonex'. The print can be left in for as long as half an hour, then rinsed in distilled water in a second dish and laid out on a sheet of glass to dry. If crease or fold marks remain, these can be treated by placing pieces of slightly damp blotting paper under the back and over the front of the drawing or print and applying gentle heat with a domestic iron. Water colours or gouaches or pastel, crayon or chalk drawings should never be washed unless by a professional.

# Sculpture

Artists and craftsmen have worked in marble, limestone, hard igneous rocks and many different woods. The first carved image or decorative detail would date from thousands of years BC. Depending on their situation many of the works have survived remarkably well. Even so, those outside may be marked by the weather of centuries, and come our industrial age even the hardest of surfaces is not proof against being attacked by rain-carrying pollutants. Moreover sculpture either of stone or wood seems in certain instances to attract the vandal, whether it be the 17th-century soldier hammering off heads from effigies or the solitary hand who in secret engraves his initials on some poor defenceless marble mantelpiece. Valuable articles can be impaired by a host of conditions: candle wax drips on to a stone bracket; a marble garden ornament stains green; the woodworm tribe sets about decimating an early Austrian carved wood saint. Furthermore these inanimate works from the sculptor's hands are all too often neglected, perched on a bookcase, or placed outside and then left. Gradually dust and grime take over and the object, perhaps just a stone pedestal with a simple capital or a piece of hard dark oak into which someone had worked an acanthus leaf, starts to lose its identity and any visual pleasure which it once gave. Many of the remedies here are quite simple and it may often prove a delight to see how these set-aside, forgotten things can come back to life.

## Materials, problems and processes

### Adhesives
Epoxy resins offer the answers to many problems for restoring pieces of sculpture; from mending small breaks to the impregnation of crumbling surfaces where wood has been riddled by

worm or perished by rot. There is a wide range to choose from (see PRODUCTS) so pick the type that states it is intended for the particular job being worked on. The epoxies really take glueing into another dimension, for you will be hard put to find something too large for them to contend with. They were employed in the saving of the great rock temples of Abu Simbel. In Poland the beams of the church of Debno-Podhalanzki were in ruin from age, rot and wood-borers; they were saved by being impregnated with epoxy resins. Full size copies of antique statues have been made using epoxies filled with such as powdered red sandstone and the finished article bears a remarkable likeness to natural stone.

The instant glues might serve for breaks with small items such as alabaster carvings or soapstone, but they would be unsuitable for large works as in many cases the surfaces to be brought together can be rough and crumbling.

Animal glues, whether hoof, fish or rabbit-skin, could be used with works in wood, but here again the epoxies will probably serve best as they are more adaptable and will accept additives more easily. (See PRODUCTS for instant epoxy and animal glues.)

## Alabaster
A type of gypsum, soft, with a fine texture and an attractive semi-opaque translucence, that has been used for carving small figures, ornaments and tablets. The colour ranges from a near-white with a slight creamy look to a light yellow ochre tint, depending on the impurities present. It will scratch very easily and also chip. Never immerse in water and soap; it is susceptible not only to the water but also to possible traces of acid that can be in tap water. Dust first and inspect the condition and, if sound, give a light wiping over with a swab of cotton wool or cloth dipped into warm soapy water and well wrung out, followed by a cloth or swab dipped into plain water and again well wrung out to remove any traces of soap. Possibly an even safer method is to use a piece of cotton wool dipped into white spirit and squeezed out. This should take off any greasy marks; dirt in details can be teased out with a brush which has been dipped in white spirit.

### Repairs
If small chips are missing or a veining has become eroded, these losses can be made good by preparing a paste of a clear contact glue with powdered alabaster (see WHERE TO GET WHAT) or gyp-

sum. If there is difficulty in obtaining these last two, kaolin or whiting can be substituted, but as these are strong white substances, minute quantities of yellow ochre or a similar dry pigment should be added. It is likely that the paste will shrink, so be prepared to make it slightly proud and then it can be carefully trimmed to shape after drying. Cleaned or repaired, the alabaster may be given a sparse coat of quality white wax polish and gently brought up with a soft chamois or cloth.

Old mends will probably have been done with an animal glue which may have darkened and looks unsightly; place some swabs of cotton wool soaked in warm water over the glue lines for a short time and they should part. Using cotton wool buds dipped in warm water, remove the old glue and, if needed, apply a little 5% solution of Chloramine T (see GLOSSARY) with cotton buds to bleach out any traces left. More cotton buds with plain water to rinse.

Reassemble using a clear contact glue.

*Stain removal*
If someone has mistaken your lovely shallow alabaster bowl for an ashtray and there are some unpleasant nicotine stains, first try cotton buds with white spirit. If this fails, try one of the fine powders, crocus or Tripoli, which are both near-white, not jeweller's rouge which has a strong reddish tint; mix up a small amount of the powder with a few drops of methylated spirits and apply the paste with a cotton bud working with a gentle circular motion. Wipe clear with white spirit then use wax polish.

**Algae or mildew, to remove**
Whether outside or indoors this green staining can quite quickly spread if neglected. In early stages it should be removed with a cloth dipped in warm soapy water to which a little ammonia has been added; rubber gloves should be worn and the piece well rinsed afterwards; or try gentle bleaching with a 2% solution of Chloramine T and rinse. For more obstinate cases see under *Poultice method of cleaning* below. Protection from this nuisance is first of all to see if the damp condition can be remedied. For an outside ornament it may be possible to do this by resetting it with some type of damp-proof course. Indoors inspect for possible sources of damp. The pieces can be wiped over if outside with a solution of 1 part pentachlorophenol to 4 parts water or indoors with a saturated solution of thymol in methylated spirits.

*Warning*: make sure there is plenty of ventilation.

## Basalt

A black rock of considerable hardness; examined under a magnifying glass it displays tiny glittering particles. Used in early periods for sculpture, and also on a fairly large scale in Egypt for paving stones, evidence the Third Dynasty (*c* 3000 BC) step pyramid at Saqquara. Layers of grime can be tackled with a stiff bristled scrubbing brush and even a wire brush. The object can be well swabbed with fairly hot water with a quality detergent and a small amount of ammonia, then worked over with the brushes and rinsed well afterwards. When dry, the surface can be treated with a 10% solution of paraffin wax (candle wax) in white spirit. Leave for about an hour, by which time most of the spirit will have evaporated leaving a coating of wax. Next with a hand butane blowlamp, set with the flame as large as it will go and still be blue, sweep the surface of the object to give a slight warming that will ensure the wax penetrates any cracks or rather soft areas. Follow with a plentiful buffing with soft cloths.

*Warning*: the paraffin wax and white spirit solution is highly inflammable.

## Breccia

A type of marble composed of angular fragments embedded in a fine matrix. When cut and polished it presents an attractive appearance and has been used for commode and table tops. The surface can be cleaned with a soft cloth dipped in warm soapy water with a small amount of ammonia; wear rubber gloves when carrying out this washing, and rinse well. Greasy marks should answer to methylated spirits, or white spirit.

## Bronzing

Plaster casts and small relief plaques or medallions have quite often been given a treatment to simulate bronze. The more subtle way is to first paint them over with a good warm brown shellac varnish to which has been added Van Dyck brown powder colour with a trace of oxide of chromium. When that is dry, highlights can be picked up by scumbling on a mixture of dark bronze powders with a thin varnish. (Scumbling is the application of an overlay of opaque or semi-opaque colour, in order to soften selected areas of the colour beneath.) If such pieces are scratched, remedy same by following the methods above that the craftsman used. It has been known for cock metal copies or fakes to be given this bronzing treatment and in the hustle and cries of a small saleroom to be taken for genuine bronzes by the unwary (see *Cock metal* under METALS).

## Consolidation
See *Adhesives*

## Flymarks, to remove
Small they may be but when on alabaster or finely surfaced white marble they must be handled with care. Don't be tempted to use a scalpel as it can be very easy to mark the surface skin. Moisten with white spirit and prise loose with an orange stick. Gently rub the area with small piece of chamois.

## Ganosis
A technique used by the ancient Greeks to soften the hard shine of polished marble. The process involved the gentle warming of the marble and then giving the surface a sparse coat of wax – they probably used a purified beeswax – and after that bringing up the desired sheen with a cloth or chamois.

## Granite
Clean and treat as for *Basalt* above.

## Insect pests
Attacks on wooden carvings can come from the woodworm, the deathwatch beetle or others that way inclined, and the trouble should be treated as described under *Woodworm* in FURNITURE.

## Limestone
Any object thought to consist of this should be carefully examined to be certain that it is really limestone and not formed of a composition. If all is well, rig up a hose so that it will play over the begrimed area, and also do this in a place where there is adequate drainage as you will need to leave the hose spraying for five or six hours. After that, turn off and attack the dirt with a stiff-bristled or wire brush; have a bucket full of water with a teacup of ammonia in it; dip the brush in and work into the mess.

*Warning*: wear gloves and goggles. The brushing will spray ammonia around, and if you drop the brush in the bucket it will splash you. Rinse thoroughly after this. If the surface that emerges appears a little friable, brush or spray on a solution of acrylic matt medium, one part medium to ten parts water.

## Marble
The light toned varieties are prone to stain very easily with rust and mildew, and also airborne mess is very noticeable when it

settles on marble. Figures, decorations, fireplace surrounds and the rest can be carefully washed with warm soapy water and if this does not bring away the grime, up to half a cup of ammonia can be added to a bucket of the washing fluid. Rinse well and dry. If stains remain, do not be tempted to use any abrasives to remove them, treat with a poultice (see *Poultice*).

## Mildew
To treat see *Poultice*

## Painted sculpture (polychrome)
Colour at one time was quite often applied to wooden carvings and to a rather lesser extent stone works. If the object is of quality, consult with the expert, for the painted areas can have many pitfalls; they will almost certainly have been touched up several times and perhaps even been altered so that it needs experience to be able to tell which are truly the original layers.

## Plaster casts
Although plaster casts often look quite robust, they can be far from it. Very easy to chip and moisture absorbent. Dust off with a soft-hair brush, not with a cloth, as the dirt may be rubbed in. If still looking rather shabby, pick up a little dry crocus or Tripoli powder (see GLOSSARY) with the brush and gently work this around on the surface, stopping frequently and dusting off to inspect progress. (See also *Bronzing* and *Poultice*.)

## Poultice method of cleaning
One of the most effective and normally the safest ways of cleaning or stain removal for stone, particularly useful with marble. A paste is mixed up of a powder called sepiolite (see WHERE TO GET WHAT) or a pulp of mashed white paper prepared, and this is applied over the stained area, or over the whole object if the condition merits it. For water soluble stains the paste or pulp should be prepared with distilled water as this will be free from impurities. The mixture should be applied as a layer about 2 cm (¾ in) thick. The principle is that at first the moisture sinks in and loosens the stain and then is drawn out again by evaporation, carrying the marks. For grease, oil or wax the paste should be made up with white spirit and used in the same way. If more drastic treatment is needed, try small additions of methylated spirits or acetone to the white spirit.

Another kind of poultice that will sometimes work with the awkward mark:

*25 g (1 oz) whiting*
*25 g (1 oz) fine pumice powder*
*50 g (2 oz) powdered washing soda*

Make this into a paste with distilled water and apply over the mark. Leave in place for about four hours (it may dry out before) then brush off and rinse surface. Any residual stains could be lightly bleached with a 2% solution of Chloramine T (see GLOSSARY) applied with a brush or piece of cotton wool, the area being well rinsed afterwards.

A more gentle poultice is to use starch mixed to a paste with hot water and put on whilst still warm; leave till dried out and brush off. Mildew stains can be treated by a poultice with water that has the addition of a little ammonia.

## Sandstone
A sedimentary rock that can have quite a fragile surface and it may be best to treat by a poultice method (see *Poultice* above). If washed, do as for limestone but omit the use of a wire brush.

## Scagliola
A composition material based largely on gypsum and isinglass and incorporating coloured marble dusts on the surface; when polished it is an effective imitation marble and was used by Robert Adam. The surface may be washed with warm soapy water, and if grime persists a little ammonia may be added; rinse and dry. Finally a sparse application of a good white wax polish may be made and then well buffed up with a chamois or sheepskin pad.

## Serpentine
Often richly coloured with deep reds, warm browns, speckled with black and at other times delicate grey-greens and near-white veining. It may be washed with warm soapy water plus a little ammonia if needed; rinse. The surface when dry has a slight greasy feel and can scratch quite easily with a hard substance. It is generally finished with a high polish by the craftsman so will not need waxing.

## Slate
Frequently used as a surround to a fireplace and consequently in many instances smoke and soot-stained. Much of this will come

away by gently scrubbing with some warm soapy liquid. If persistent, a white spirit poultice (see *Poultice*) should bring the grime away.

A rather more drastic course: following the safety precautions outlined below, apply a 5% solution of hydrochloric acid, made up by a chemist, on some waste cloths after masking off surrounding materials. Leave wet with the acid for about 30 seconds and then liberally rinse with several waters.

*Warning*: wear good rubber gloves, avoid splashes on exposed skin and also clothing, and protect eyes with goggles.

If after cleaning, the slate has a miserable look, treat it with a mixture of white spirit and boiled linseed oil in equal proportions. This is best applied with a lump of cotton wool inside a couple of thicknesses of cotton rag; be sparing and rub well in.

## Soapstone
A soft stone somewhat like alabaster that has been used for making small carvings. It is best treated in a similar manner to alabaster.

## Stain removal
See *Algae or mildew, Flymarks, Poultice* and under appropriate material.

## Wax figures
Just about the easiest things to damage when being cleaned. If of rarity, pass them straight along to the professional. If not, make the first cautious approach by just dusting over with a soft-hair brush. If dirt still remains, work in with the brush very small quantities of fine pumice powder mixed with plaster of Paris. If the object is coloured, you will have to be very careful not to remove the colour.

## Wood carvings
When badly soiled and clogged with dirt they can be brushed over with the liquid suggested under *Grime* (see page 30). Work it well into the details with a stiff brush and then rinse away with white spirit. See also under *Adhesives* and *Insect pests*. Never finish with varnishes, plain, tinted, gloss or matt, because they will be out of sympathy with the material. Put on a sparse application of beeswax polish (see page 21) or good white wax polish and give plenty of buffing with a soft cloth, chamois and fairly large soft brush to get into the details.

# Miscellany

To list everything that comes under this heading would be almost an impossibility but below is a selection that sets out to be representative of the whole field. It includes a round-up of those objects and techniques that cannot really fit into the preceding chapters. Many of these could be classified as bygones.

As antique prices have climbed and saleroom cupboards have emptied of usual lines a fashion for the things of yesterday and the day before has grown. There are some items that may or may not be tomorrow's treasures but are eminently collectable today. Small intimate objects of the home, concerned with domesticity, leisure, and those bits and pieces that made up the lives of our near ancestors. In fact, where does one draw the line for bygones? In some cases it almost seems as though as soon as something is no longer generally obtainable, it's collectable.

The trouble is that with many of these objects you may have to start looking after them from scratch as no one may have considered them worthy of care when they were still in use.
were still in use.

### Antlers
Our immediate forbears seem to have spent considerable energy pursuing and killing, spurred on by the prospect of getting their prowess written into the record books for size and species. If antlers are just mounted with perhaps a part of the frontal bone straight on to a wooden plaque they should not be much trouble. Broken pieces are best put back with the help of an epoxy adhesive (see PRODUCTS), joint surfaces being first well cleaned and degreased with methylated spirits; if small portions are missing, make up a paste with the epoxy or a contact adhesive, plus some whiting and powder colour to match in. The whole antlers can be washed with a cloth dipped in warm soapy water and a little ammonia, rinsed off and dried. Finish with a white wax polish which will bring up the colours of the horn.

If, however, the antlers come complete with the head and a fair stretch of neck, it could be a longer and messier job. Examine the fur, ears, eyes and mouth to see what state they are in. If sound, give the fur a good cleaning by sprinkling on potato flour or fuller's earth (see WHERE TO GET WHAT); work this in and then brush out. If there are any signs of moth, make sure this is cleared and then apply a proprietary protective preparation. If the skin round the ears etc is perished it can be consolidated with acrylic matt medium (see GLOSSARY), or a treatment with the leather dressing on page 114 can do much to revitalise it. To improve the look of 'starved' fur it can be given the absolute minimum of greasing. Put a fingertip's touch of vaseline in the palm of one hand, rub both hands together so that there is only a suspicion on each and then stroke them over the fur once it has been brushed into the correct lay.

## Barometers
If they are not working when acquired or suddenly cease, don't fiddle with them, take straight to the expert. The cases, however, can be given some attention; if in a dirty condition, apply the cleaner mentioned under *Grime* on page 30. Be careful that it goes only on the woodwork, and put it on with a small swab of cotton wool. Leave for a few minutes and then wipe off with more cotton wool dipped in white spirit. Brass strip decoration should be masked off from the wood and then cleaned with a proprietary polish. Inlays of bone or mother-of-pearl, also being masked off, can be brought up by applying 20 vol. hydrogen peroxide or a 2% solution of Chloramine T (see GLOSSARY); rinse with swabs moistened with water. Polish whole case with white wax polish.

A careful inspection of the mercury bulb at the bottom of the tube may save trouble. Lay the barometer face down on a table and unscrew the back and prise off. This should expose the chamois membrane which seals in the mercury and rests on the small plate that is lowered or raised to adjust setting. If the chamois shows signs of perishing it is best, once again, to take it to the trained hand.

## Battersea enamels
A method developed by Stephen Theodore Jannsen around 1750 at York House in the London district of Battersea. His production only lasted for a few years as he went bankrupt. Versions of the ware were made later at Bilston and Wednesbury in Staf-

fordshire. The real objects are rare indeed; principally they were trinket and snuff boxes. Made of copper, they were surfaced with a kind of opaque glass that may have been decorated with transfer or hand painting. The safest cleaning method is the use of lukewarm soapy water, which should be applied with a squeezed-out swab of cotton wool and wiped off with another moistened with clean water. Any solvents, even the mild white spirit, should be avoided. Finish off the cleaning by polishing with white wax polish.

### Blue John

A variety of fluorspar of violet-blue colour, often with yellow veinings, that is found in Derbyshire and is also known as Derbyshire spar. It has been made into many decorative objects; these quite often have metal mounts that may be ormolu or bronze. When cleaning, particularly the ormolu, be very careful that the liquids suggested under *Ormolu* in FURNITURE do not get on to the Blue John as they could attack and stain it. Mask off the stone with adequate strips of Sellotape. A further precaution can be to make a small collar of a roll of rag and tie this round the neck of the object just below the metal mount.

The Blue John itself may be washed with cloths dipped in warm soapy water to which a few drops of ammonia have been added, rinsed and then dried with towelling. The surface skin obtainable with this material is one of its most attractive features and should be treated with care as some specimens will scratch quite easily. A finish with white wax polish may be given and this will also tend to hide any small abrasions or scratches.

### Bottles

These may range from fine crested and dated examples down to tiny pill and cordial bottles from the Victorian apothecary. The first move should be to clean them out thoroughly as some might even after the years have unpleasant and possibly dangerous trace elements inside. A hot solution of 25 g (1 oz) of borax to 600 ml (1 pint) water will shift most things; if not follow up with a 2% solution of hydrochloric acid, made up for you by the chemist. With cork or stopper in place, swirl the solution round in the bottle and leave for about ten minutes, then pour out and rinse well. Stubborn deposits can be worked at with a stiff bristled bottle brush.

*Warning*: wear rubber gloves.

Corks and rubber washers may well have perished and it is acceptable to replace these with new ones which can be 'aged' with a little staining and perhaps the use of a piece of sandpaper. Breaks are best attended to with an instant glue (see PRODUCTS) after the surfaces have been cleaned and degreased.

## Buckles

The late Victorian era and the following period were great times for fancy buckles on shoes, clasps to belts and the like. These might have been made from one of many different low cost alloys and decorated with paste-gems, enamels or engraving. Examine first to see how firm any decoration is and if all is well, start by cleaning with cotton buds dipped in white spirit, and also use a small brush. One of the proprietary dip type cleaners (see PRODUCTS) can be tried for bringing up the metal parts; rinse afterwards. A proprietary polish can be worked over the metal with a cotton bud and subsequent to buffing with a cloth or chamois a light application of white wax polish will give some lasting protection.

## Buttons

As with buckles there was an amazing proliferation of buttons at the same period. Fabric covered ones if sound can be put in a jar with some white spirit and given a gentle swilling around for about five minutes, then pour off the spirit and spread the buttons out on a plate to dry where there is good ventilation.

*Warning*: fire risk.

Horn, bone and like substances may be put into a jar with a couple of handfuls of potato flour, given a good shaking up and left for several hours. Repeat shaking and leaving two or three times then sift out the buttons. To finish, put a few drops of almond oil on to a clean rag, work it about till evenly dispersed and then roll the buttons around in the rag. Metal ones may each have to be laboriously cleaned with a polish, and they can be given a coat of lacquer last thing.

## Cameras

Unless you are a camera mechanic, leave the innards to an expert. But much can be done with general cleaning. Lightly moisten a cotton bud with a few drops of white spirit and with this, remove dust from wherever you can see it externally and also from metal parts when the front is let down and the lens is exposed. Be careful if there are brass parts as these may have the original lacquer on and this should be preserved. Leather covering the body and cases can be treated with the dressing mentioned on page 114. Any loose parts can be stuck back again with an adhesive marked as being suitable for leather and metal or leather and wood.

## Clocks and watches

As with barometers, let the professional handle mechanical and all troubles to do with the insides. If you enter these parts you may get a shock as 'marriages' can be quite common in certain areas of the horological world. Be content with cleaning the case. If dirty, use the liquid suggested under *Grime* on page 30. When cleaning inlays, mask off the wood. Finish with a white wax polish. Some clock cases have ventilation slots, generally covered with fretted brass, and behind these should be small flaps of velvet or similar material to act as filters to remove dust from the air. These filters may be missing or rotted; replace if required. Brass dials can be carefully cleaned with a paste made from crocus or Tripoli powder (see WHERE TO GET WHAT) with methylated spirits; it should be worked into details with cotton buds or a small brush. The metal surface can then be treated with a white wax or lacquer.

Watches should have just the case cleaned, using a method suitable for the particular metal (see METALS). All other matters leave to the watchmaker.

## Cooking pots and pans

Some of these may be so soot covered and dark that it will be nearly impossible to tell what they are made of. Drastic measures are called for. Immediate grime can be brushed over with a hot solution of sodium hydroxide (caustic soda), 25 g (1 oz) to 4.5 l (1 gall), left for a couple of minutes and then scrubbed with a stiff-bristled brush.

*Warning*: wear rubber gloves and goggles and take care to avoid splashes.

Copper pans may then be treated with an appropriate dip type cleaner (see PRODUCTS) and can be finished off with proprietary polishes or a paste made up of jeweller's rouge and methylated spirits. The insides may be tin-lined and if caked with remains of past recipes, pour in hot water with half a cup of washing soda, leave for five minutes, pour off and rinse. Again, wear rubber gloves for such doings. Iron pots are likely to be rusty; treat with a proprietary rust remover (see PRODUCTS), agitate with steel wool and rinse well with paraffin. Copper can be lacquered for display; iron given a thin coat of lanolin or white wax polish.

## Corkscrews

Until you start collecting such things it is not appreciated just how many different types there are. They can have bone and wooden handles, small brushes, be plated, and sometimes have small silver plaques engraved with the owner's name or crest. Steel parts: see under *Iron* in METALS. Silver plaques can be wiped with a cotton bud moistened with a dip preparation (see PRODUCTS). The bone should be wiped off with warm soapy water with a few drops of ammonia added. When dry it can be swabbed with a 2% solution of Chloramine T (see GLOSSARY) and rinsed. The brush should be gently washed with soap and water and rinsed and left lightly tied with a piece of tape whilst it dries so that the shape will be retained.

## Dolls

Ceramic faces and limbs can be washed carefully with small pieces of cotton wool dipped into warm soapy water and squeezed dry. Residual grime can be tackled with a cotton bud dipped in dry potato flour, being careful over facial colour which may not be glazed in but applied after. Hair, if stuck on, may also be cleaned with potato flour: gently work it into the hair and then brush out. I know a famous north country doll museum where the good lady runs an almost non-stop laundry service for her charges. In strict rota they are stripped to the buff or whatever a doll's equivalent is, and sit beside the tub whilst every stitch is given the treatment. See TEXTILES for instructions on washing the different kinds of material.

## Fans

Examples of fans dating from well back into history may be found. Versions of them were used by the Assyrians, early Egyptians and Greeks. Early fans were generally of the broad-bladed type mounted on to a staff. The early Church used a type called a *flabellum* to keep flies away from the altar at the time of Mass. Craftsmen have expended much imagination and skill on making these rather fragile objects, and materials are diverse: papers, parchments, silks, cottons and feathers have formed the fanning surface; the sticks have been made from various woods, bamboo slivers, mother-of-pearl, tortoiseshell, bone and ivory. Applied decoration has been made with gold and silver. Fans have been painted by artists and have sometimes included a small spyglass set into the handle.

*Cleaning methods*
If the surface of the fan is firm it may be cleaned by gently caressing with a piece of art gum or a lump of new bread. Bone or ivory sticks can be given a careful bleach with a 2% solution of Chloramine T. Silver may be treated with a proprietary dip preparation. Tortoiseshell will respond to a little white wax polish. Feathers can be dusted with potato flour and gently brushed free of the powder.

A really beautiful fan is best today kept purely as a display item. It should be opened out and mounted in a glazed frame.

## Flat irons
These commonplace items have recently been promoted from the laundry room to display shelves around the house. A number come in quite exotic shapes with long handles; sometimes, if they were heated by charcoal, they have little chimneys and can bear an amazing variety of makers' names. If badly rusted they can be shot-blasted (see WHERE TO GET WHAT) and then given a light coat of white wax polish or lanolin; lesser rusting can be treated with a rust remover (see PRODUCTS).

## Food pots or cosmetic jars
Often quite beautifully decorated with pictures and lettering, they used to contain preparations such as bear's grease, pomades, pastes, preserves and tooth powders. If stained, they can be treated quite freely with 20 vol. hydrogen peroxide or a 5% solution of Chloramine T (see GLOSSARY); rinse well. Breakages can be put right with an instant or a contact adhesive, not forgetting to clean and degrease the surfaces to be joined.

## Hair
In the 19th century there was a fashion for making bracelets, necklets and rings from horsehair. Human hair was also used and mementoes of dear ones turned up in the back of lockets, with locks entwined in intricate patterns. If the object made from hair does not have other material with it, it should be safe to swish it around in warm soapy water and then rinse and place to dry on an absorbent surface such as a piece of towelling. If the item feels greasy, gently rinse it through some white spirit and set to dry. If it appears 'starved' after this, rub in a minimum of

almond oil and wipe off any excess. With lockets it is just possible that a moth could have got at the hair, so to cut out any risk of this, give a small spray with a saturated solution of thymol in alcohol.

## Hairdressing equipment

Gadgets here can include the really old-fashioned type of hair tongs and their accompanying heating devices; treat as for the particular metals as suggested in METALS. One person I know captured what must be among the first of all hood hair dryers and after treating amongst other things, copper, chrome plating, glass, iron and brass turned the thing into a standard lamp. Another collector I heard of had picked up such a rarity as an American Virginia stool shower which had been in use around 1835; it has a revolving seat, a lever to pump water up to the shower-rose, which at the same time moved a scrubbing brush up and down the user's back. It could nearly be classed as a shampooing outfit. Glazed earthenware parts of hairdressing bygones could be scoured with crocus powder (see GLOSSARY), water and a few drops of ammonia.

## Horn

This has been used for a variety of objects, split and flattened for early 'horn' books, as a shield for some early lanterns, as drinking vessels, handles for cutlery, combs and snuff and trinket boxes. It may be treated as for *Tortoiseshell* (see page 131). Abrasions and scratches can be removed by using the 'rubber' with a paste of crocus or Tripoli powder (see GLOSSARY) mixed with methylated spirits and then the surface afterwards treated with a few drops of almond oil or the whole given a sparse application of white wax polish and brought up with a chamois. Breakages can be made good with an instant or a contact glue

## Jelly moulds

The cooks years back called for far more imaginative moulds than those we slavishly submit to today. Copper, glass and china were modelled into splendid fishes, birds and animals. Copper moulds can be treated with a dip type cleaner and stains removed with a home-made 'rubber' (see page 83) and a paste of jeweller's rouge or crocus powder with methylated spirits. Glass if grimed inside can be left soaking with a solution of borax, 25 g (1 oz) to 600 ml (1 pint) water, for about half an hour; and the outsides, if the objects are to be displayed, can be wiped over with a rag dipped in methylated spirits. China if cracked and stained should be freely swabbed with a 2% solution of Chloramine T or 20 vol. hydrogen peroxide, and rinsed.

## Knife handles

A common casualty with tableware is that the bone, horn, ivory, mother-of-pearl or wooden handles become detached. The cause is too often close proximity to steaming hot water. The original glues would have been animal, fish or shellac based. Use a slender skewer or similar rod with some kind of edge on it to scrape out all the residue of the former glue and any cement that may have been used (*see diagram 18a*). Clean off the glue and cement from the spike at the end of the blade, fork or spoon. Mix up a fairly liquid paste with some kaolin, marble dust (see WHERE TO GET WHAT) or whiting with a contact glue or an epoxy. Try to get a little of this right down inside the hole of the handle then add a little more all round the spike (*see diagram 18b*) and push the covered spike into the hole in the handle (*see diagram 18c*). Gently ease it with slight wriggling motions so that it seats right down into place. Wipe off any excess that has been squeezed out (*see diagram 18d*) and leave to set for at least 24 hours. Really good quality tableware should always be washed individually; it should never be put right into the water.

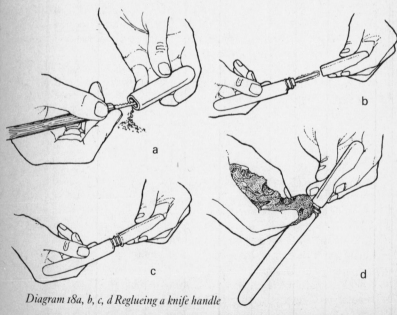

*Diagram 18a, b, c, d Reglueing a knife handle*

## Magic lanterns

Treat with the same respect internally as cameras (see above) but go over the main body and other external metal and wood parts to deter rust and incipient corosion. Watch out for original lacquer on brass parts.

## Money boxes

Materials used can include: cast iron, treat as for *iron* in METALS; brass, use a proprietary polish and treat stains with a 'rubber' (see page 83) and paste of jeweller's rouge with methylated spirits; printed tin plate, little more is needed than a wipe over with a rag dipped in white spirit; wood, white wax polish; ceramics (if still in one piece, it is a feat to have found it), clean outside with a cloth and warm soapy water.

## Musical instruments

With these, unless you are a musician who understands them, stay clear other than to polish the outside of the grand piano with white wax polish. Don't even be tempted to start on metal fittings, or trying to remove scratches from the backs of violins. All this is for the specialists.

## Noah's arks

These may be of the dozen best known animals variety or one of those splendid examples that came from Bavaria around the middle of the last century with upwards of 150 pairs of animals, birds and insects, from elephants down to ladybirds. Many may need new legs, ears and tails; these can be supplied fairly simply. Buy some different thicknesses of dowel rod. Shape new limbs whilst rod is still in the length (easier to hold), then cut off (*see diagram 19a*). Push a thin pin half into the body of the animal (*see diagram 19b*) and add a touch of glue and force the new leg down on to the other half of the pin and into position against the body. When the glue has set, brush a thin coat of gesso over the new wood and next day paint to desired colour and when dry, varnish (*see diagram 19c*).

## Office equipment

Things such as old typewriters, punches, staplers, guillotines, addressing die-stamps and desk phones have moved from the utilitarian to the nostalgic scene. Best treatment with all these is to give a thorough clean up with rags and brushes and white spirit; a lens blower can help to get dust out of awkward corners.

169

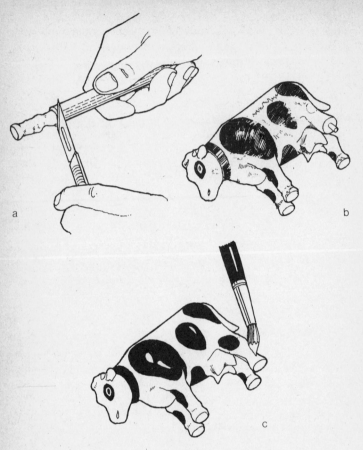

*Diagram 19a, b, c Repairing a Noah's ark animal*

Working parts can have the old oil sluiced out with paraffin and fresh fine oil dropped in. Decorated enamel and gilt surfaces may be given a thin coat of a good white wax polish and buffed up.

## Paper
Grouped under this heading can come items such as greeting cards, instruction manuals, magazines, newspapers, pamphlets, posters, programmes, tickets and so on. Many of them, because they will have been printed on wood pulp or esparto grass paper,

will probably have browned and darkened quite considerably with the years. They may respond to bleaching by the following method. Experiment with one of the least favoured examples by laying it in a flat dish of 2% solution of Chloramine T and leaving it for up to half an hour. Pour off the bleach solution, rinse in clear water and leave to dry on a piece of white blotting paper.

## Pests

Amongst these items, particularly if they have a binding or fastening involving animal glue, you may meet a strange weeny fellow that looks under a magnifying glass a bit like a tiny lobster. This will be the firebrat who likes well-dried glues and pastes and bindings; living nearby may also be silverfish and book lice. If infiltrated material is put in an airtight tin or box with a little paradichlorobenzene all three of these vagrants will be effectively destroyed.

## Papier mâché

A term for objects made from mashed-up paper or small sheets of layered paper mixed with a size, shaped in a mould, varnished, decorated, given a coat of shellac and, after hardening in a japanning oven, polished.

Papier mâché has been used for items as large as bedheads, painted panels on coaches, down to trays, table-tops, trinket and snuff boxes. The trays and tabletops, in particular, are often damaged by having hot liquids spilt on them or over-hot objects placed on them. This can cause the protective layers of lacquer to crack and the exposed material is very prone to damage by damp. The best cleaning for them is to use white wax polish on a piece of cotton wool or soft cloth and finish with a chamois. If the woodworm is around, include papier mâché in any inspections, as the tiny brute is quite partial to a slight change of diet. If discovered, treatment can be a little difficult as spirit-based killers can affect the material. For safety the objects should have a fumigation. A polish incorporating an anti-woodworm ingredient is safe to use.

## Pens

Old fountain pens generally suffer from dried ink clogging everything. In most cases the whole pen can be left soaking in warm water with a little borax for at least half an hour. After this the old ink should rinse away. Bodies and caps of the pens can be brought up with white wax polish.

## Plastics

We might tend to think that making things of plastics is something that has come upon us in the last thirty years. But wrong. In 1855 Alexander Parkes, a Birmingham inventor, is said to have developed the first commercial plastic which was known as Parkesine. Since then a range of these synthetic materials has come from the coal, agricultural, and petrochemical industries. Jewellery, dressing table accessories, glove stretchers, hot water bottles, cups, snuff boxes and wireless cabinets are but a few of the torrent of items that have been moulded, and extruded by the factories. Plastics may be washed with warm soapy water plus a few drops of ammonia. Grease and oil may be wiped off with a cloth dipped in white spirit. Keep acetone well clear as this could dissolve some plastics quite quickly. Breakages should be repaired with a contact glue named as intended for these materials.

## Scientific instruments

Treatments permissible with these are limited. Leather dressing (see page 114) for the shagreen cover of microscope and telescope barrels is safe. Be very careful with the brass fittings, as they may retain the original lacquer and this should not be disturbed. Working parts can be gently cleaned with a cotton bud dipped in white spirit and fresh lubricating oil put where needed. If rust is noted, apply a remover with a cotton bud; leave on for the prescribed time and rinse off with paraffin. Wooden cases should be watched for woodworm (see *Woodworm* in FURNITURE). They should also be cleaned with the liquid recommended under *Grime* in the same chapter, then have a white polish applied and be shined up with a soft cloth or chamois.

## Skins

If of value, send to a trained furrier. The fur side can be cleaned by sprinkling heavily with heated potato flour (see WHERE TO GET WHAT); the skin should then be rolled up and placed under some old blankets, preferably with some hot water bottles and left to stand for about four hours. Remove blankets, unroll skin out flat and gently brush out potato flour.

## Stoves

The kinds can range from simple basket grates to Cornish slab ranges and ornamented cast-iron turtle stoves. Rust will be the main enemy; depending on the amount, it may be treated with a liquid remover or shotblasted (see WHERE TO GET WHAT). If cracked, send to be professionally mended. Those that are not enamelled can be stove-blacked.

## Stuffed birds and animals

Feathers and fur can be treated with warmed potato flour; leave on for a few moments and then brush off. The specimens are best moved from their settings for treatment. Quite a little licence may be taken with the settings; parts may be replaced if withered, backgrounds can be repainted. After the stuffed one is put back and before resealing the glass case, put in some insect pest repellent, paradichlorobenzene or thymol.

## Tools

In a workroom or suchlike, arrangements of the tools of a trade on a wall, rather in the manner of how our great-greats put up swords and firearms, can look quite well. The choice is varied: shipwrights', gardeners', thatchers' and those associated with dairywork. After being de-rusted or de-tarnished, metals can be lacquered or given a white wax polish. Woods after being inspected for worm attack can be treated with teak oil and buffed to a medium sheen.

## Toys

Mechanical toys may need rust treatment; after that they can be gone over with cotton buds dipped in white spirit. Painted or enamelled parts should be given a thin coat of white wax polish and then carefully buffed up with a soft cloth or chamois, being careful not to catch any little fragile pieces that stick up. Working parts can be given a few drops of fine oil.

Games boards may be cleaned with a piece of art gum or a lump of fresh bread. Bone dominoes, spillikins and that sort of thing can be given a light bleaching in a dish with a 2% solution of Chloramine T and then rinsed. Where loose corners are flapping, go round with a soft brush and a water-soluble glue or paste and bed them down.

## Tunbridge ware

Small boxes and other little objects decorated with a miniature inlay technique using an extraordinary number of woods such as amboyna, ash, birdseye maple, blackthorn, cherry, laburnum, mulberry, plane, rosewood and Spanish chestnut (see page 15). The inlays can be prone to damage by damp; if any raising is noticed it should be dealt with at once. Prepare a little rabbit-skin or hoof glue in a liquid state and flood this on to and into the surface of the object that is in trouble. Take a piece of greased paper and lay it on the top and leave a heavy weight such as an old iron on top of this for at least 48 hours. Remove the iron, pull off the paper and, with a swab of cotton wool dipped in warm water, wipe off any excess glue. Then resurface with white wax polish and give a gentle but brisk buffing up with a chamois.

## Vinaigrettes

These may be of glass or metal with a perforated top to hold smelling salts or a small sponge with some liquor that would give off reviving vapours. Wearing rubber gloves, wipe over with a little methylated spirits to which a small amount of ammonia has been added, and also rinse out interior with the same liquid. Sluice out with water and dry interior with a hair dryer. Metal vinaigrettes can be cleaned as appropriate to the type of metal (see METALS). Hinges should be cleaned and re-oiled; metals can be lacquered.

## Wire, barbed

There are apparently some 300 types of barbed wire and it is becoming a speciality collector's item. Rubber gloves are not of value here but rather those huge thick leather ones that are used by hedgers. What do you do when you get hold of it? I'm not quite sure! Except, go through the rust removal process and if your hands are still serviceable after that, finish off with a light coat of lanolin.

# Security

There may not be a Rembrandt, a Paul Storr silver bowl, a Kashan rug, or a diamond necklace in the house, but that doesn't mean your home is immune to the attention of the thief concerned with antiques. Humble brass candlesticks, domestic china of the Edwardian times and 1920s, domestic bygones, are all currency for him.

Burglaries are running at more than 800 every single day of the year throughout the country. Statistically, three out of four people are liable to robbery at least once in their lifetime. Two out of every three burglaries are committed by teenagers. So great is the amount of 'merchandise' removed that it is impossible for the security services to prevent or indeed to detect every likely occurrence, and then to recover the goods. Items stolen in Cornwall could well be on sale quite openly forty-eight hours later in the north-east or be (by one ruse or another) shipped speedily across to the Continent; and if they land there the chance of the owner regaining his lost treasures will be slim indeed.

The robber today is no respecter of persons, situations or even of the cloth. Not long ago a couple of 'bent knockers' casing the south of Ireland visited a convent and persuaded a novice nun to show some of the convent treasures. On hearing that the convent was short of money for new curtains, they then persuaded her to part with old and rare valuable silver spoons and creamers for a minimal price. In another location a number of well-instructed thieves using hefty bolt cutters, which incidentally can be bought in many toolshops, sheared off protective steel bar grids, entered a window and stole seventeen ancient silver chalices. Nowhere is really safe. The Pro-Cathedral in Dublin has recently had a four-camera surveillance system installed, not only as a control against undesirable visitors, but to protect donation boxes and the treasures of the building. One of the more audacious crimes of this nature occurred in Italy. Very determined art thieves arrived in a large pantechnicon at a small church in the north. They entered and bound the priest, who was the only person in the building, barricading him into a confessional box, and then removed a rare triptych and drove away.

One of the strange factors about the thefts of rare antiques is that all too often when the account is read, it is quite clear that the thieves knew what they were after; they enter a building and select certain items, thus indicating that somewhere there must have been a master mind (and a very well-instructed mind) not only in the history of art and antiques but also with a very useful list of possible 'fences' and buyers for the trophies. It is also noticeably rare for a fake to be stolen, although it is not unknown for some of the more cleverly 'distressed' reproductions to deceive the crook.

But does all the blame lie on the side of the burglar? Not really, because the large majority of householders take absolutely minimal precautions; in fact, they almost seem openly to invite intrusion. All too many are apathetic to the problem, probably answering a trembling conscience with 'it won't happen to me'. The proverbial stories of full milk bottles left outside the front door when the occupants are on holiday, newspapers stuffed into a letterbox and unremoved day after day, do occur. Keys are left hidden under flowerpots, foot-scrapers, doormats. The crook learns about such things from his first primer. All too many occupiers have identification and address tags on their personal key rings – lose them and you present the thief with an easy opportunity. Gossip columns often inadvertently advertise that 'so and so' will be away in the south of France for two months. Crook spies at auctions can note who buys what, and then decide where it will be fairly safe to have a try. All this may sound elementary, tiresome and almost to be scoffed at, but the crook lays his plans initially often on the merest whispers of information.

With inflation, the average value of house contents today – just for quite humble and simple objects – can tot up to an often surprising figure. Isn't it worth spending perhaps ½% of that value to provide resistance to intrusion which will scare off over 90% of the villains and persuade them that it is easier to try somewhere else? Undoubtedly, of course, if a gang has selected some objects in your house they are absolutely determined to get hold of, there has yet to be devised a system which can totally defeat their entry. They can go to security exhibitions, they can make enquiries just as you can, they have their experts who are working all the time to keep one step ahead of the security device manufacturers – who are working just as hard to keep a step ahead of them.

How many people moving into a new home take the simple precaution of installing new locks all round? How many take the care to choose multi-lever locks for all the outside doors, make sure the doors and windows fit tightly, install window bolts? How many take the trouble to have some means of identifying an unexpected caller, ask for identification from a visiting service person? How many keep toolsheds, garages locked, ladders safe inside, and remove other obstructions which can be used to assist a climb-in? How many casually reveal their telephone number and address to unknown callers?

Walk down a street, a village or town, and how often can a casual sideways glance show beautiful pieces of silver, china, glass displayed proudly on shelves or tables right in front of or easily seen through a window? A sure welcome for the visiting Bill Sykes.

Police analysis of the burglar's initial attack is enlightening. Strangely enough, Friday often seems to be the chosen day. In one area where there was a total of 285 break-ins, nine were attempts on the basement, 257 on the ground floor, and nineteen on the first floor. Points of entry in the majority of cases were through a rear window, then followed the front door, the rear door and a front window. The large majority of entries were made in daylight.

Most criminals will be shy of noise or undue delay when the jemmy or other instrument doesn't almost instantaneously effect a break-in. That ½% expenditure on security devices mentioned earlier will easily cover the necessities to provide an effective perimeter defence. Adequate and strong locks should be fitted to doors, locks and bolts to windows – sash windows being particularly vulnerable. If the building is being restored and the window frames replaced, see that they are made with the glazing rebate on the inner face. For easy 'break-in' windows there are a number of laminated glasses available which will resist very heavy objects and even blows from sledge hammers. Add to the above a good stout door chain that will allow just a couple of inches opening and a peephole through the door – make sure with the latter that you get one that has very wide acceptance angle – and finally consult your local police crime prevention officer, and you could be well on the way to achieving peace of mind and holding on to your treasures.

# Devices and procedures

## Alarms

On the market today are a great number of systems that cover very nearly any security situation. They range from a simple micro- or other type of wave intruder detector, up to sophisticated devices that appear almost human in the way they can differentiate between various types of movement, whether the intruder is human or animal, or branches shaking with the wind, also there are those that can detect minute changes in temperature.

In some ways the detectors that work off batteries and thus have no vulnerable wires are most suitable for a private house. A number of these are skilfully designed to give the appearance of antique cabinets. The most sensitive can detect human movement within a fifty-foot radius and when activated sound a siren that can be heard up to 250 metres away in the open. These micro-wave instruments work on the same principle as radar speed detectors. There are anti-theft protection systems which use the most advanced technology and enable an entire system to be completely self-contained in one cabinet. The batteries last for three months in continuous operation, and unlike many micro-wave devices the frequency used enables it to detect human movement through brick walls, plasterboard, wooden partitions, windows and doors, and circuitry is incorporated to eliminate responses from other physical disturbances.

Variations of defence by these electronic wizards can include specific protection for a single object or a series of treasures. They can be set to watch the main entry door. They can also be set to have short delay periods between detecting and sounding off the alarm. Some of them may have simultaneous switches that will set off external audio and visual warning devices. Another related type is one that listens; it is an acoustic alarm which can cover most of the rooms in the house, providing all the internal doors are left open.

Whatever type of alarm is chosen, that detail of having a delay from the alarm system picking up the intrusion to sounding off is vitally important because if it sounds as soon as it picks up the intruder, it is unlikely that there is a chance of apprehension. If there are a few minutes' delay, it does allow a chance for the security forces to appear in time.

## Doors

With older properties it is quite possible that the doors of good stout oak, beech or pine, and of a sturdy thickness, as fitted by our ancestors, will still be adequate, unlike some of the weaker items which may be fitted to houses today. Often these frail things may be a bare 30 mm (1½ in) thick, being sometimes only tempered hardboard on a wooden frame, and perhaps half or even two-thirds glazed, making them a simple proposition for the intruder. It may be pleasant to have extra daylight in the hall, but from the security angle it is begging for trouble. To discourage the first tentative probings for entry, don't rely on just a rim night-latch or spring plunger with a bevelled head. They offer little resistance to even semi-skilled ruffians. Go for a multi-levered mortised deadlock; have it set right into the door itself, not screwed on to the back, and if more thorough protection for that front door or back door is needed, have a system which when locked not only pushes a bolt across but pushes bolts out of the top and the bottom of the door into heavy metal sockets. With an outfit like that, the door will almost have to be shattered before an entry can be made.

If the door and its surround as standing is weak in any part then extra security is needed. There are specially constructed security doors and frames that include insurance-approved, five-levered deadlocks and reinforcements of not only the woodwork but also the hinges and hinge bolts. Some of these have an amazing strength, and will take a pressure of over three-quarters of a ton on the lock area without failing.

As mentioned earlier, a few pounds spent on an efficient spyhole or door-viewer can be a comfort, especially for those living alone. Many of these are so small that when they are fitted underneath the bottom of a knocker or other door furniture, they are practically invisible. It is important to pick one with at least 160° angle of vision through the lens, and also with a small internal shutter that can be pulled across the viewer to prevent unwelcome eyes outside seeing inside.

A step up from the spyhole is a video door-phone. This enables you to identify the caller without even going up to the door. Within three seconds of the caller pushing the button outside, you will have a clear picture of him or her, day or night. When the button is pressed, a light comes on outside which enables an ingenious miniaturised hidden camera to deliver the picture to your monitor unbeknown to the caller. It can also be used as a check-sentry for investigating strange noises outside the door; just switch on and it will be possible to hear and see what is going on outside.

## Electronic tags
These have been used for some time in large stores to protect against shoplifting, but variations of them can be of use for protecting specific items in a collection. The modern tag is generally a very small plastic-covered device which, in conjuction with a separately sited pick-up beam, will raise the alarm if the objects are moved. These small gadgets have devices that ignore other sources of quite normal interference caused by such as transistor radios, hearing aids and other electronic gadgets.

## Individual tremblers
There are small devices which can be fitted unobtrusively on to window-glass, window-frames or doors, and which will become activated if any attempt is made to force an entry that causes vibration. These small guardians generally consist of an amplifier, a microphone and vibration contact. For antique and art objects there are trembler devices that can be fixed to the frames or stretchers of pictures or to pieces of furniture or the display cases. They will give round-the-clock protection, and can be activated by even the smallest interference or movement of the object which they are protecting; sounding off if there are attempts to cut a canvas from its frame or to interfere with their own wiring system. These may be applied to single objects or it is possible to have a circuit which will serve up to six or more.

## Home security packs
There are available a number of 'do-it-yourself' kits. These are battery operated and have at their centre a small control unit which will activate an alarm. This can be triggered by a device on a door or a window, or by a pressure pad, or the operation of a personal attack button, and also by any unauthorised attempt to tamper with the system.

## Light, mist and noise
Perhaps somewhat sophisticated and sounding rather formidable, there are systems available for those living in isolated houses which can be triggered off by a device set in the perimeter wall, fence, gate or door, which as soon as an intruder is detected will switch on very powerful floodlights, let off an intense, shrill sound alarm and as a final deterrent release what is

described as an instant dense cloud of artificially-created fog. All three combined are more than enough to give even the most determined criminal a desire to remove himself from the area as speedily as possible.

## Personal alarms

For the person who is alone in a house and could encounter an intruder, there is a remarkably effective shrill alarm which is about the size of a handbag-perfumaire. It has a pushbutton control and if directed straight at the intruder, lets fly with a non-toxic non-inflammable gas-activated shriek of about 110 decibels, enough to upset the character's hearing and senses for long enough for an escape to be made or even to drive him to escape himself.

## Pressure pads

These devices are usually about 60 cm × 30 cm (2ft × 1ft) and are quite thin. The intention is that they should be fitted underneath carpets or in concealed places on stairs, inside doors, inside windows, and other places which could be used by the intruder. They would be linked up to one or other systems of the general alarms. If concealed properly, they can be remarkably effective, because however carefully the thief will have opened the window or door, he may well become over-confident and sound off with a carefully placed pressure mat.

## Records

It is a wise policy to have in the inventory of possessions details that can assist the police in recovering objects in the event of theft. These should include written descriptions of the important items and notes of any small damages, such as chips, heavy scratches and dents, that will help in identification. Small sketches, as well as colour prints or transparencies should be included. If possible, take the photographs yourself, as the less publicity your possessions have the safer they will be.

## Windows

Whether sash, metal or wooden casements, or sliding patio french windows, all need some form of extra security. The simple and speedily fixed window-bolt can be remarkably effective and will give considerable protection. It may be fitted on to the frame itself or with casement windows on to the latches. There are also locks available for almost every type of window.

Ordinary window-glass offers practically negative protection, but today there are laminated safety glasses which are extremely impressive. This laminated glass can be fitted either into windows or doors or if there is a specific very special treasure, it can be incorporated into the picture frame or display case, and a further plus is that some of these glasses have a built-in ultra-violet ray protection. A window will resist heavy attacks by thrown bricks, crowbars or sledge hammers, and multi-ply laminations will resist multiple attacks by revolvers, rifles and shotguns. Even explosions will not cause the terror of violently broken glass showering the place with sharp fragments. The pieces adhere to the interlayer of special plastic.

The personal treasures we accumulate are worth care and security. The alternative to spending a small fraction of their value on their protection is to lock them away in a bank vault or heavily protected safe; thus seemingly defeating the object of having them.

# Products for Cleaning, Polishing and Treatment

There are a number of products specially developed for professional use with antiques which are available from a firm which has co-operated with leading British conservators and has the approval of the British Museum. All the products listed below can be obtained in small packs from Picreator Enterprises Ltd, 44 Park View Gardens, Hendon, London NW4 2PN.

**Renaissance wax polish**
A micro-crystalline wax cleaner/polish that gives excellent results on wood, leather, metal, marble, stone, shell, ivory, plastics and even paper. Recommended for use wherever 'white wax polish' is referred to in the text.

**Renaissance leather reviver**
Revitalises dry leather. A lanolin based product with long-term protection against insects and bacteria.

**Limousine wax polish**
A micro-crystalline wax polish with added inhibitors of metal corrosion and leather mould.

**Pre-lim**
A mildly abrasive cream for safe, non-scratch removal of oxidised grime and stains from many surfaces.

**Vulpex liquid soap**
A non-foaming germicidal cleaner for a wide range of materials from textiles and carpets to metals and stone. Uniquely soluble in water or white spirit.

**Groom/stick**
Permanently tacky rubber; an 'everlasting' dry non-abrasive cleaner for picking up many kinds of soiling marks from firm

surfaces of all kinds, especially paper. Degreases dirty hands, removes fingerprints from silver etc.

### Mystox LPL
Insecticide, fungicide, bactericide (ie long-term moth-proofer and eliminator of mildew bacteria). Protects all natural-fibre textiles, carpets, leather, wood and paper.

### Calaton soluble nylon
Invisibly strengthens fragile paper and various materials; consolidates weak, fraying textiles.

### Texicryl 13-002
Acrylic emulsion used as an adhesive, size, consolidant, surface coating, paint improver and high load medium for dry pigment colours.

### Stadex WS 503
Refined, pre-cooked starch powder producing instant cold water heavy duty adhesive paste; pH neutral.

Specialised products may also be obtained from House of Harbru, Common Lane, Industrial Estate, Doncaster Road, Wath-upon-Dearne, Rotherham, South Yorkshire Tel: 0709 874887. Send 50p for catalogue and information sheets, which will be refunded with first order.

They produce a variety of materials for working on metals, furniture and other categories, including: French polish, button polish, knotting, sealers, goldsize, paint removers, wood dyes, brass and copper polishes and cleaners, shellacs, wax polishes, wax filler sticks, polish reviver, clock case restorer, silver polish and silver cloth jewellery care kits, tarnish removers.

Frank W. Joel Ltd, Hardwick Industrial Estate, Kings Lynn, Norfolk, supplies useful specialised equipment and chemical preparations.

## Adhesives

*Safety rules*
Always follow the manufacturer's instructions; adhesives can be dangerous if used incorrectly.
The strong smell of some adhesives can cause headaches and dizziness so work in a well-ventilated area.

Many adhesives are inflammable so don't smoke and don't work near a naked flame such as a pilot light.

Keep adhesives out of reach of children and pets.

N.B. Wherever possible carry out an initial test on a small sample to check that there is no adverse reaction before proceeding with the main repair.

A wide range of adhesives is stocked by most DIY, hardware and department stores. Buy in small quantities, enough for the job in hand, as they can deteriorate. If you have difficulty in tracing a suitable adhesive you can contact the following firms for details of their products. Most include several types of adhesive within the range.

**Araldite adhesives**
CIBA-Geigy Plastics Division, The Technical Department, Duxford, Cambridge, CB2 4OA
*Tel*: 0223 832121

**Borden adhesives**
The Humbrol Consumer Products Division of Borden (UK) Ltd, Marfleet, Hull, HU9 5NE
*Tel*: 0482 901191

**Bostik adhesives**
Bostik Ltd, Consumer Division, Ulverscroft Road, Leicester, LE4 6BW
*Tel*: 0533 50015

**Copydex adhesives**
Copydex Ltd, Consumer Services Department, 1 Torquay Street, London, W2 5EL
*Tel*: 01-286 7391

**Duro lines**
The Rawlplug Co Ltd, Technical Advisory Services, 147 London Road, Kingston Upon Thames, Surrey, KT2 6NR
*Tel*: 01-546 2191

**Evo-stik adhesives**
Technical Service Department, Evode Ltd, Common Road, Stafford, ST16 3EH
*Tel*: 0785 57755

## Loctite adhesives
Loctite (UK) Ltd, The Public Relations Department, Watchmead, Welwyn Garden City, Herts, AL7 1JB
*Tel*: 96 31144

## Polystik adhesives
B. Cannon & Co Ltd, Kingston Grange, Hopwood Lane, Halifax, West Yorkshire, HX1 1ET
*Tel*: 0422 50231

## Reeves adhesives
Reeves, Works Chemist, Lincoln Road, Enfield, Middlesex, EN1 1SX
*Tel*: 01-804 2431

## Uhu adhesives
Beecham Uhu, 11 Stoke Poges Lane, Slough, Berkshire, SL1 3NW
(Letter enquiries only)

## Unibond adhesives and sealants
Unibond Ltd, The Technical Advisor, Tuscam Way, Camberley, Surrey, GU15 3DD
*Tel*: 0276 63135

# Animal glues

### Rabbit skin glue/rabbit skin substitute glue
Winsor and Newton supply art shops with a rabbit skin substitute glue. This is available in granular form, to which water is added for use.

Robersons Ltd, 71 Parkway, London NW1 (01-485 1163) sell a rabbit skin substitute glue, again in granular form. They have a small shop and mail order system from the above address, as well as supplying art shops.
Quantity: available in 450 g (1 lb) quantities.

John Mylands Ltd, 80 Norwood High Street, West Norwood, London SE27 (01-670 9161) also supplies a rabbit skin substitute glue by mail order.
Quantity: available in 450 g (1 lb), 3.2 kg (7 lb), 6.3 kg (14 lb), and 12.6 kg (28 lb) quantities.

## Hoof glue/non-specific animal glue

As a specific glue this is difficult to obtain, but there are non-specific animal glues, which are made up of undetermined ingredients, all of natural origin which one could use as a substitute. Available: John Mylands Ltd (see above).

## Fish glue

Frank Romany, Ironmongers, 52 Camden High Street, London NW1 (01-387 2579) sell fish glue in granular form.
Quantity: available in 450 g (1 lb) packs.

# Detergents and soaps

## Teepol

Concentrated detergent for general household jobs. Cash and Carry outlets.

# Furniture polishes

**Aerosol polishes**

| | |
|---|---|
| Antiquax Wax Polish | Antique dealers, hardware shops |

**Cream polishes**

| | |
|---|---|
| Stephenson's Olde English Furniture Cream | White beeswax polish; department stores, hardware shops |

**Paste wax polishes**

| | |
|---|---|
| Antiquax Fine Furniture Polish | Natural or dark brown for light or dark woods; antique dealers, hardware shops |
| Colron Finishing Wax | Antique dealers, hardware shops |
| Goddard's Cabinet Makers' Wax | Some hardware shops and grocery outlets |
| Kleeneze Antique Furniture Polish | Contact Kleeneze Limited, Hanham, Bristol for your local agent |

| | |
|---|---|
| Lily White Wax Polish | White wax polish; hardware shops |
| Mansion Wax Polish | Light or dark; supermarkets, hardware shops |
| Rentokil Wax Polish | Contains silicones, but also insecticide to protect against woodworm attack; hardware shops, department stores |
| Simoniz Original Fine Wax | Car accessory shops |

## Furniture treatments and repair products

| | |
|---|---|
| Antiquax Furniture Cleaner | For removal from polished wood of old wax and grease build-up; antique dealers, hardware shops |
| Cuprinol Teak Oil | For natural finish teak, afromosia and rose wood; paint and hardware shops, supermarkets |
| Joy Scratch Dressing | Light or dark; suitable for most polished wood surfaces, including French polish; do-it-yourself and hardware shops |
| Kleeneze Teak Oil | For all hard woods when an oiled surface is required; contact Kleeneze Limited, Hanham, Bristol for your local agent |
| Rustin's Teak Oil | Suitable for cedar and all bare woods; for indoor and outdoor use; do-it-yourself and hardware shops |
| Topps Scratch Cover Polish | Light, medium or dark; hardware shops, department stores |
| Topps Teak Cream | For solid teak and other solid hard woods; hardware shops, department stores |
| Topps Teak Oil | As above |

| | |
|---|---|
| Topps Teak Oil Spray | For all teak and hard wood veneers; hardware shops, department stores |

## Glass

| | |
|---|---|
| Hagerty Chandelier Cleaner | Applied as a spray and left to dry |

## Gold leaf

| | |
|---|---|
| Geo. M. Whiley The Runway, Station Approach, South Ruislip Middlesex | Also other metallic leaves and foils |

## Hand protection

| | |
|---|---|
| Marigold Husky Gloves | Resistant to grease and oils; cotton lined, pliable, ribbed for gripping; most department stores |

## Jewellery

| | |
|---|---|
| Goddard's Jewellery Care | Dip cleaner for gold, silver, platinum and also precious and most semi-precious stones; jewellery sections of department stores, jewellers, silversmiths and some hardware stores |
| Hagerty Jewellery Care Set | For diamonds, gold, silver and pearls |

# Lacquers

| | |
|---|---|
| Knobs & Knockers Clear Lacquer | For metals; also sold in a set together with Lacquer Stripper and Corrosion Remover; all Knobs & Knockers shops |
| Rustin's Transparent Lacquer For Metal | Gives up to ten years protection to the newly cleaned surface of brass and copper; do-it-yourself and hardware shops |
| Solvol Clear Protector | In aerosol form for use on chrome, stainless steel and other bright metals following cleaning and corrosion removal; motor accessory shops |
| Specialist | Gedge & Co Ltd 88 St John Street Clerkenwell, London EC1 |

# Leather

| | |
|---|---|
| Carr's Leather Oil | For softening and waterproofing leather; leather shops |
| Carr's Leather Stain | Available in several colours; leather shops |
| Connolly Cee Bee Hide Food | For use on all finished leathers; leather shops |
| Leafood | For use on finished upholstery leather; mail order only from Bridge of Weir Leather Co. Ltd., Clydesdale Works, Bridge of Weir, Renfrewshire, Scotland |
| Leathers (mostly sheep) | J. E. & R. F. Hann, 8 Limerick Close Milborne Port, Sherborne, Dorset |

| | |
|---|---|
| Hopkin & Williams Leather Dressing | For leather covered books and desks but not upholstered furniture; originally formulated for the British Museum. Potassium Lactate is recommended for initial treatment and is also available from Hopkin & Williams Ltd., Freshwater Road, Chadwell Heath, Essex |
| Properts Leather & Saddle Soap | Department stores and supermarkets |

## Metal polishes and anti-tarnish treatments

| | |
|---|---|
| Bluebell Polish | For brass and copper; department stores and supermarkets |
| Bluebird Silver Polish | For gold, silver and crystal; some hardware shops |
| Brasso | Polish for brass, copper and copper alloys |
| Day & Martin Metal Polish | For brass, copper and other metallic surfaces; some hardware shops |
| Duraglit Metal Polish | Impregnated wadding for cleaning brass, copper and copper alloys |
| Duraglit Silver Polish | Impregnated wadding for cleaning silver, aluminium and chrome |
| Goddard's Long Term Silver Foam | Water soluble polish. Particularly suited to ornate pieces as it is applied with a sponge and rinsed clear, so leaves no deposit |
| Goddard's Long Term Brass & Copper Polish | Gives a more lasting protection against tarnishing |
| Goddard's Long Term Silver Polish | Gives a more lasting protection against tarnishing |

| | |
|---|---|
| Goddard's Silver Dip | For the removal of stains and tarnishing from cutlery and small items |
| Hagerty Copper Wash | Applied with a sponge and rinsed clear |
| Hagerty Metal Polish | For stainless steel, brass, copper and chromium |
| Hagerty Silver Care | Water soluble polish; applied with a sponge and rinsed clear, so particularly suited to ornate items |
| Hagerty Silver Clean | For the removal of stains and tarnishing from cutlery and small items |
| Hagerty Silver Duster | Impregnated to renew the anti-tarnish barrier to newly cleaned items |
| Hagerty Silver Guard | Protective bags, pocketed rolls and wraps for anti-tarnish storage of silver items |
| Hagerty Silver Keeper | Vapour releasing cartridge for imparting anti-tarnish protection to items stored in drawers and cabinets |
| Hagerty Silver Spray | For protection against |
| Hagerty Tarnish Preventing Silver Polish | tarnishing (Hagerty products are available from jewellers and jewellery departments of leading stores) |
| Hermetite Metal-Brite | Polish with no abrasive content; for aluminium, brass, copper, silver and stainless steel; hardware and motor accessory shops |
| Hermetite Ali-Clean Multi-Purpose Aluminium Cleaner | For removal of dirt, tarnish and corrosion; Halfords and Woolworths |
| Hermetite Ali-Clean Aluminium Finishing Cream | For restoring finish to aluminium, chrome and stainless steel |
| Johnson Chrome | Polish for chromium; garage accessory shops |

| | |
|---|---|
| Polivit Silver Cleaning Plate | For use with washing soda in hot water for tarnish removal from immersed items. From jewellers, hardware stores, chemists and antique shops |
| Silvo | Polish for silver, EPNS, aluminium and chrome |
| Tarnprufe | Protective bags, rolls and wraps for anti-tarnish storage of silver items; Harrods, John Lewis Partnership, Mappin & Webb or by mail order from Tarnprufe Co. Ltd., 30 Sidney Street, Sheffield 1, Yorks |
| Town Talk Silver Foam | Applied with a sponge and rinsed clear, so particularly suited to ornate items; jewellers |
| Town Talk Silver Plate Powder | Used in conjuction with methylated spirits or water and recommended by the manufacturers for antique silver; Harrods Pantry Department |

## Moulds and damp

| | |
|---|---|
| Bondaglass-Voss G4 Damp Seal | For sealing walls and floors against penetrating damp; ship's chandlers and some do-it-yourself shops |
| Doulton Wallguard | This firm offers a damp proofing service and the Doulton Wallguard dehumidifier for domestic situations. Details from Doulton Wallguard Ltd, Unit 6, Ashville Trading Estate, Bristol Road, Gloucester |

| Rentokil | This firm markets Fungo mould inhibitor for domestic use. Also offer a range of damp proofing treatments. Details from Rentokil Ltd, Felcourt, East Grinstead, West Sussex |
| Westair dehumidifier | Details from Westair Dynamics Ltd, Central Ave, East Molesey, Surrey |

## Paintings

| Robersons Picture Wax | A surface protection which is an alternative to varnish |
| Winton Picture Cleaner | To remove grime safely; available from art shops |

## Pest control products and services

| Cooper | Aerosol Mothproofer also effective with carpet beetle and Fly Killer also effective with silverfish; chemists, hardware and grocery shops |
| Cuprinol | Products for eradication of woodworm and protection against further infestation; details from Customer Service Unit, Cuprinol Limited, Adderwell Rd, Frome, Somerset |
| Rentokil | Pest control, woodworm and dry rot services and products; details from Rentokil Limited, Felcourt, East Grinstead, West Sussex |

## Rust remover and lubrication

Jenolite Rust Remover — For the removal of rust from iron and steel; hardware stores, do-it-yourself and car accessory shops

## Security firms

Brocks Alarms — Large range of alarms devices, tags and integrated systems

Chubb Alarms Ltd — Comprehensive range of protective systems for the home

Gateway Security Systems — Protective devices against burglary and vandalism

Geemarc Ltd — Video doorphones

Group 4 — Full list of all types of device from simple alarms to the most sophisticated

Ingersoll — Door and window locks

Philips — Do-it-yourself home security kits

Rhino Securities Ltd — High security doors and frames

Safe and Sound — Locks, door and personal alarms

Security & Commitment Systems Ltd — Micro-wave intruder detector devices battery run

SMP Security Ltd — Wall and floor safes

## Security glass

Monsanto Ltd
   10–18 Victoria Street
   London SWIH ONQ — Laminated glass giving high protection from guns, sledgehammers and thrown bricks

# Stain removal

| | |
|---|---|
| Beaucaire | Liquid remover for grease, tar and oil-based stains on carpets and upholstery; large branches of Boots |
| Dabitoff | Liquid remover for grease, tar and oil-based stains, particularly suited to use on clothing; large branches of Boots, hardware and department stores |
| Goddard's Dry Clean | Aerosol for grease stains; also aids removal of sugar-based and water-based stains |
| K2r Stain Remover Spray | Aerosol for greasy spots and stains on clothes, carpets, upholstery and wallpaper |
| Holloway Carpet Care Spot Removing Kit | Four solvents for the removal of a wide range of stains from carpets; G. E. Holloway & Sons Ltd, 12 Carlisle Road, London NW9 |
| Holloway Chewing Gum Remover | Aerosol for use on carpets and upholstery (not for delicate fabrics); available as above |
| Movol | Liquid rust remover for white cotton fabrics; large branches of Boots or in case of difficulty direct from Movol Products Ltd, 66 Harrow Lane, Maidenhead, Berks |
| Thawpit | Liquid remover for grease based and other stains on clothes, carpets and upholstery; grocery, chemist and hardware shops |
| White Wizard | All purpose cleaner and spot remover in soft paste form suitable for use on fabrics, carpets, upholstery and hard surfaces; Harrods and most |

House of Fraser stores or in case of difficulty contact AMS, 21 Queen Street, Blackpool, Lancs

## Stone care

| | |
|---|---|
| Bell 1966 Cleaner | Powerful cleaner for use on stone; will remove plaster and cement from the surface |
| Belsealer | For sealing the surface of all porous stone |
| Bell Special Marble Cleaner | Bell products available from A. Bell & Co Ltd, Thornton Road, Kingsthorpe, Northampton, Northants |

## Stoppers

| | |
|---|---|
| Brummer Stopping | In two grades for interior or exterior use; standard wood colours; hardware and do-it-yourself shops |
| Brummer Rub-in Woodgrain Filler | For interior use; good colour range; available as above |
| Joy Plastic Wood | In natural pine, dark oak, mahogany, teak and walnut for interior and exterior use; hardware and do-it-yourself shops |
| Joy Wood Filler | In natural colour only; available as above |

## Strippers

| | |
|---|---|
| Joy Paint Stripper | For removing cellulose, emulsion and oil based paint, |

| | also French polish and varnish; paint, do-it-yourself and hardware shops |
| Joy Takesitoff | For removing Joy Transparent Paint and repolishing the metal; do-it-yourself and hardware shops |
| Knobs & Knockers Corrosion Remover | Also removes verdigris and tarnish from metals; all Knobs & Knockers shops |
| Nitromors Water Washable Paint Remover | For emulsion, oil based and cellulose paints, varnishes, lacquer, French polish; semi-gel consistency makes it suitable for vertical surfaces and carvings; on delicate wood wash off with white spirit to avoid raising the grain; do-it-yourself and hardware shops |
| Ronstrip | For paint removal from wood |
| Polystrippa | For removing some types of varnish and most paints |

## Textile assistance

| Association of British Launderers and Cleaners 319 Pinner Road, Harrow, Middlesex HA1 4HX | Customers Advice and Conciliation Service |

## Textile cleaning products

| 1001 Dri-Foam | A liquid concentrate, non-rinse carpet shampoo |
| Bissell Extraction Shampoo | For use with the Bissell Deep Clean carpet cleaning machine |
| Bissell Foam Carpet Shampoo | A liquid concentrate, non-rinse carpet shampoo for |

| | |
|---|---|
| | use with Bissell electric or hand operated carpet shampooer; can be hand applied |
| Bissell Upholstery Kit | A liquid concentrate shampoo and foam generating applicator |
| Bissell De Luxe Upholstery Kit | Aerosol shampoo with clip-on roller head applicator |
| | Bissell products stocked by hardware shops, Co-op stores, department stores, some grocery outlets |
| | Bissell electric carpet shampooer and the Deep Clean machine can be hired from independent hardware stores and hire shops |
| Holloway Chewing Gum Remover | G. E. Holloway & Sons Ltd, 12 Carlisle Road, London NW9 0HZ |
| Service Master First Aid Kit 50 Commercial Square Freeman's Common Leicester LE2 7GR | Contains chemicals not normally available for treating a wide variety of stains |

## Veneers

| | |
|---|---|
| Art Veneers Co Ltd Industrial Estate Mildenhall Suffolk IP28 7AY | Large selection, also adhesives, waxes and clock movements |

# Where to get what

**Abrasive powders** (crocus, emery, pumice, tripoli, jeweller's rouge)
*Some art shops, especially those dealing with metal plate printing supplies; ironmongers; jewellers*

**Acids and other chemicals**
*Chemists; most will be willing to make up required strengths but give warning as a little time will be needed*

**Acrylics** (medium, colours)
*Art shops*

**Alkyds**
*Messrs Winsor & Newton and most art shops*

**Armenian bole**
*Art shops*

**Beeswax**
*Chemist*

**Burnishers** (agate, bloodstone)
*Art shops*

**Carpet cleaner with insecticide**
*Ironmonger*

**Casting-resins with metallic fillers**
*Alec Tiranti, 21 Goodge Place, London W1*

**Chloramine T**
*Chemist*

**Cuttlefish**
*Pet shop*

**Dry powder colours**
*Art shop; lower grades from a decorator*

**French chalk**
*Chemist, ironmonger*

**Fuller's earth**
*Chemist, ironmonger*

**Fumigation bomb or candle**
*Ironmonger, sometimes chemists*

Glaze substitute
*Varni-Das, the product referred to on page 54. Art shops, dealers in craft materials especially those for pottery*

Hydrogen peroxide
*Chemist; 20 vol. will generally be stocked*

Kaolin
*Chemist or shops specialising in pottery supplies*

Marble dust
*Art shops specialising in materials for sculptors. Alec Tiranti, 21 Goodge Place, London W1*

Oil of spike
*Chemist or art shop*

Potato flour
*High class grocers, some chemists*

Proprietary pastes for ceramic repairs
*Ironmongers, some art shops*

Saponin extract
*Chemist (who might have to order this specially) or good herbalist such as Culpeper*

Sepiolite
*Chemist*

Specialised adhesives, consolidating materials (leather, metals, ceramics, glass, woods)
*Ironmonger, do-it-yourself shop*

Shot blasting
*Ironmonger, some garages, metal workshops*

Whiting
*Ironmongers or decorators*

# Glossary

*Abrasives*
In the sense used throughout the book this term implies fine powders that may be employed, either dry or mixed to a paste with water or methylated spirits, to remove stains from metal or as a polish. These include: emery, putty, *Crocus* and *Tripoli* (see separate entries).

*Acetone*
A strong solvent for varnishes and waxes. Highly inflammable with a strong smell, toxic to many. It should only be used where there is adequate ventilation.

*Acrylics*
A group of polymers or copolymers of acrylic acid. Artificially prepared resins that are used as vehicles with colours for painting, and also as a medium and a varnish. Useful for consolidating loose surfaces.

*Alcohol*
A useful but highly inflammable solvent; also used as a vehicle with polishing and abrading pastes. A Customs permit will be needed before making a purchase; these are not freely granted and do not guarantee success. *Methylated spirits* is more easily obtainable and is suitable for most purposes.

*Ammonium acetate*
This can be used as a neutraliser after cleaning lead corrosion with weak hydrochloric acid. It should be applied as a very weak solution and then itself rinsed off with plenty of water.

*Ammonium thiosulphate*
A 15% solution of this with water plus a few drops of quality detergent may be used to clear extreme tarnish. Rinse off thoroughly afterwards.

*Benzene (or Benzol)*
On no account use this solvent, which is obtained in the distillation of coal-tar or synthetically. It is highly inflammable and poisonous. Do not confuse with *Benzine,* see below.

*Benzine*
A spirit similar to petrol, also highly inflammable. Useful as a cleaner for fabrics and as a solvent for most resins, varnishes and waxes.

*Bloom*
A misty look, similar to the bloom on a grape, that comes up on polished surfaces. It may be on the top of a polish or a varnish, or underneath; if the latter, it is difficult to remove because the varnish or the polish will have to be taken off first. Cause is probably connected with cold and damp, possibly at the time of the application of the polish or the varnish.

*Bole, Armenian*
A red clay that can be placed under gold leaf when it is being laid, the idea being that it will assist in enriching the appearance of the fragile gold leaf.

*Bronze powders*
Any metal, as copper or aluminium, reduced to a fine powder and tinted to be used as a pigment for a paint. The range available includes gold tints from pale to deep, silver, copper, brass, pewter, tin and a number of reds, blues, and greens with a metallic look. They can be mixed with varnishes, acrylics or adhesives.

*Carbon disulphide*
Very effective woodworm and other insect pest destroyer, but not recommended for use by the amateur as highly poisonous and inflammable.

*Carbon tetrachloride*
Solvent for oil and grease on textiles. Once widely used and often an ingredient in proprietary stain removal preparations but its use in the home is not recommended as it is highly poisonous.

*Carcass wood*
The framework or support timbers for veneers and inlays.

### Chloramine T
A mild bleaching agent in the form of a fine white powder which is to be dissolved in water (preferably distilled); a 2% solution is most commonly used. It has the advantage that the bleaching property is soon lost and that after rinsing nothing harmful remains.

### Crocus powder
One of a group of abrasive powders obtained from metals by calcination. It is so called in reference to the purple colour that results from one of its constituents, ferrous oxide, being burnt. Particularly valuable for removing scratches from metal, it has many other uses.

### Electrotyping
A technique for producing a copy of a metal object. It was developed by Jacobi and success was reached in 1838. It involves the depositing of a metal in a cast taken from the original model by a form of electrolysis; the thin deposited layer is then usually backed by a baser metal for support.

### Enamel
Powdered glass to which metallic oxides have been added to provide a variety of colours. These mixtures are placed on the surface of metals and fused, which causes them to vitrify and adhere to the metal surface.

### Formaldehyde
A powerful fumigant, antiseptic and preservative. The vapour is poisonous so that if it is necessary to use it considerable ventilation should be provided.

### Glair
A traditional adhesive used for laying gold leaf on to a gesso ground that has been brushed over with Armenian bole (see above). It is egg white beaten up with a little water.

### Glaze
Vitreous coating of ceramics. It can also be a transparent coat of colour put over a painting or a polished surface to give a translucent tint effect.

*Hydrochloric acid*
Despite its many uses for cleaning and restoring, this should only be obtained made up in the prescribed dilution by a chemist as it is a dangerous acid that gives off fumes that can cause eye damage. For handling this and other acids see warning note on page 6.

*Hydrogen peroxide*
Diluted with water it is a reasonably safe bleach. It is obtainable in various strengths and 20 vol. is the one recommended most commonly in this book. It should be stored in a dark-coloured glass bottle in a closed cupboard to keep its properties. Analytical reagent grade should be bought as this will contain no harmful stabilisers.

*Impasto*
In ceramics the term refers to decoration formed by thick layers of coloured slips, giving a raised effect to the pattern.

*Japanning*
The art of giving a high-gloss finish to woodwork and metal objects. The fashion for this glittering finish began in the latter part of the 17th century. When japanning was applied to metals the technique involved baking between each application of the shellac varnishes.

*Marouflage*
The method for attaching paintings to a wall by certain adhesives. It is also applicable to the fixing of detached painted decoration on textiles to wood supports in cabinet-making.

*Methylated spirits*
Wood alcohol that has been denatured by the addition of methanol, pyridine and a violet dye. If it is felt the colour is going to be a trouble with a particular method a few drops of ammonia will generally remove it.

*Oxalic acid*
A poisonous acid, sold in the form of white crystals, which is used in weak dilutions for stain removal and other purposes. It should be obtained from the chemist ready made up in the required dilution. See warning note on page 6.

## Paradichlorobenzene
Generally purchased as white crystals which give off a vapour highly poisonous to insect life; it works best if slightly warmed and in a sealed area. When handling, provide plenty of ventilation.

## Polychrome
Applied to sculpture, it means that the object is or was painted.

## Repoussé
The method for decorating metal by hammering and punching from the reverse side.

## Rottenstone
A much weathered limestone which is rich in silica, when powdered it is used for polishing metal, either as a dry powder or as a paste mixed with water or alcohol.

## Sodium hydroxide (caustic soda)
Strong solutions are used as a wood finish stripper; diluted it can serve as a stain remover or reducer. Not an acid but quite as dangerous, being highly corrosive and poisonous. Great care needed when handling; protect eyes and skin. See also warning note, page 6.

## Sodium perborate
When well diluted, a reasonably safe mild bleach for treating textiles.

## Thymol
Useful as a mild fungicide and insect pest deterrent. It dissolves in alcohol and also in ether. It has an aromatic odour, being obtained from the oil of thyme.

## Tripoli powder
A fine abrasive powder so called because the fossilised alluvial deposit from which it is produced was originally found near Tripoli. It is chiefly used for polishing metals.

## Weeping glass
A condition which can afflict Roman and other antique glasses. It is caused by the presence of too much alkali; drops of potassium carbonate appear running down the surface. Treatment by an expert only.

*White spirit*
Also known as turpentine substitute, it is a mild solvent distilled from petroleum. Can be used as a diluent for powerful solvents, and as a stain remover, particularly with those stains caused by oils and grease. White spirit is inflammable.

*Whiting*
White chalk that has been ground up and washed. May be used as a polish for metals, either as a paste with water or alcohol or as a dry powder. Useful when mixed with adhesives as a filler for many purposes.

# Index